Super Saints Book III

D1553170

Defenders
of the
Faith

Saints of the Counter-Reformation

Bob and Penny Lord

Journeys of Faith®
1-800-633-2484

Books by Bob and Penny Lord

This Is My Body, This Is My Blood
Miracles of the Eucharist - Book I

This Is My Body, This Is My Blood
Miracles of the Eucharist - Book II
The Many Faces of Mary, a Love Story
We Came Back to Jesus
Saints and Other Powerful Women in the Church
Saints and Other Powerful Men in the Church
Heavenly Army of Angels
Scandal of the Cross and Its Triumph
Martyrs - They Died for Christ
The Rosary - the Life of Jesus and Mary
Visionaries, Mystics and Stigmatists
Visions of Heaven, Hell and Purgatory
Trilogy Book I - Treasures of the Church
Trilogy Book II - Tragedy of the Reformation
Trilogy Book III - Cults: Battle of the Angels
Super Saints Book I - Journey to Sainthood
Super Saints Book II - Holy Innocence
Super Saints Book III - Defenders of the Faith
Este es Mi Cuerpo, Esta es Mi Sangre
Milagros de la Eucaristía
Los Muchos Rostros de Maria una historia de amor

ISBN 1-58002-134-4

Defenders of the Faith

Table of Contents

I.	Dedication	iv
II.	Introduction	6
III.	St. Philip Neri	9
IV.	St. Francis de Sales	29
V.	St. Jane Frances de Chantal	53
VI.	St. Vincent de Paul	61
VII.	St. Charles Borromeo	97
VIII.	Popes of the Counter-Reformation	119
IX.	St. Robert Bellarmine	149
X.	St. Ignatius of Loyola	165
XI.	St. Teresa of Avila	195
XII.	Bibliography	220
XIII.	Index	221

Dedication

In times of crisis, God sends us Powerful Men and Women to defend the Church. Our Lord has always loved our Church. Whenever it seems the powers of hell are going to devour His Church, He calls Defenders of the Faith to protect His Church. This book is about love, the love these Saints had for their Lord and His Church.

The Sixteenth Century came and Satan felt he had the Church by the throat and he was going to choke her to death. This book is a tribute to those who stood up and fought against the powers of hell so that we, four hundred years later, have a Church. It is also to those who helped us to first have the courage to write this Trilogy - Mother Angelica and her Nuns, and to those of the different communities and shrines who helped us immeasurably gather accounts of these heroes' lives.

We want to dedicate this book to:

Pope John Paul II - our Shepherd, our *"Sweet Christ on Earth,"* for giving us the courage to go bring you the lives of our ancestors, those Saints who stood on the Words of Jesus, and defended those Words with their lives. Our Pope, John Paul II, is a man for all seasons, a Defender of the Faith, unparalleled in the History of Our Church. We praise You, dear Lord Jesus for him, and ask you to protect him and keep him strong and healthy.

Mother Mary Angelica - our inspiration, a sign in the Church and the world that Our Lord has not abandoned us. In this new time of challenge and trial, God has given us another Powerful Defender of the Faith and Role Model to challenge us when we are too weary to go on, to fight the impossible fight. We thank her for affirming our Ministry in our daily walk to bring the people of God, Role Models to give us hope and help to steer the Ship of the Church to port. Lord, we thank you for her and the *Poor Clares Nuns of Perpetual Adoration* at Our Lady of the Angels Monastery in Birmingham, Alabama.

Luz Elena Sandoval and *Brother Joseph* - Our Spiritual children - without their zeal and loyalty, none of this could happen. We thank Our dear Lord Jesus for them, and ask Him to continue to bless them, give them strength of body and soul, and keep them in the palms of Your Hands.

The Custodians of *La Chiesa Nuova, Rome Italy* - the shrine of St. Philip Neri. They gave us background on the life of the Saint for our book and television program, most especiallly the time in which the Saint ministered to the Faithful, the period of the Counter-Reformation.

The Family of St. Francis de Sales and members of the Order of the Visitation in Annecy, France - for the background help and guidance in sharing the life of the Archbishop of Geneva, St. Francis de Sales, and the co-foundress of the Visitation Order, St. Jane Frances de Chantal. We also thank the custodians of the shrine of Our Lady of Loreto in Italy for sharing on the time St. Francis spent at the Holy House.

The Custodians at the Cathedral of Milan, Italy - final resting place of St. Charles Borromeo, for their assistance in gathering all the information we needed for this chapter, as well as their aid in videotaping the Cathedral, to bring you the television program which comes from this story. We are also grateful for the custodians of the *Borromeo castle in Arona, Italy,* for allowing us to visit and videotape his birthplace.

The Jesuit Community, including *Fr. Joseph Fessio in San Francisco, California,* and *Fr. Harold Cohen in New Orleans, Louisiana,* for their help with our four Jesuit Saints in this Trilogy, and also for the help of the Jesuits at the Gesù in Rome, and the Apartment of St. Ignatius Loyola next door to the Gesù.

The Daughters of Charity in Paris, France - both at the Chapel of the Miraculous Medal on the *Rue du Bac,* and the Church of St. Vincent du Paul on the *Rue de Sèvres,* for their help in bringing you the life of their father-in-faith, St. Vincent de Paul, for our book and television documentary.

We thank Our Lord Jesus for all of you! We love you!

The days of Saints and Sinners

Who will defend our Faith?

How do you write about those chosen to live and die for the Church? We had to do a great deal of praying; the lives of these *Defenders of the Faith, Saints of the Counter-Reformation* filled us with joy and pride to be Catholic, but also with awareness of the role Our Lord is asking all of us to play, in this the days of **Super Saints** and Deluded Sinners.

It was so reassuring, so affirming to read about our Pope's strong stand on who is Catholic and who is not, admonishing those calling themselves Catholic theologians, professors in Catholic institutions, priests, bishops, religious and laity that they are required to teach, according to the Magisterium or cease claiming they are teaching under the authority of the Catholic Church; further stating that those dissidents who teach other than the teachings of the Church are not Catholic but heretics.

In this book, *Defenders of the Faith*, you will read about those in the Sixteenth and Seventeenth Centuries who pretended to be Catholic and instead were teaching heresy, leading innocent lambs astray. Because of this 6,000,000 souls never knew what happened; they awakened one day and discovered they were no longer Catholic. Will that happen to us? The Pope cries out, *Halt! Cease and desist!* We cry out, *No more lies! No more heresies packaged in fancy wrappings to deceive us!*

As never before, we must be an educated people. The most important education, and yet the shortest one, the most neglected one, has been the very learning that could save our souls, the souls of our families and those of the world, that of our Faith and those who came before us, the Saints.

In this world of deceit and delusion, where we don't know who to believe, we need to read about Heroes and anti-heroes; we need to learn about Saints and sinners. Our book is about heroes who fought anti-heroes and earned the Crown of Victory and the Dove of Peace for the Church. Our book is about Saints and Sinners. Our book is about the past speaking to the present and then to the future! Our book is about faithfulness, right up to the Cross! Jesus told His disciples, *"If any man would come after me, let him deny himself and take up his cross and follow Me. For whoever would save his life for my sake will find it."*[1] These Saints took up their crosses and followed Him, losing life on earth for a greater eternal life with Him in Heaven. And yes, my brothers and sisters, there is a Heaven.

Possibly no time in the History of the Church and the world have we been so close to losing lives and souls. Oh, nations have been under attack in the past, with almost whole continents standing on the edge of a precipice of annihilation; but never has the world faced total destruction. Because of the hi-tech global telecommunication of today, the evil that man does in the darkness of his soul, is soon broadcast throughout the world, affecting millions of people. We can hear the Lord crying out, *Whom can I send to save My children from inevitable slaughter?* For He has always summoned people like you and me, to go out and defend His Church and save the innocent lambs who could be lost, without someone to bring them the Truth, Who is Jesus.

In this day of Saints and sinners, where we are so often confused, we do not know Saints from sinners, we need to know the Saints of the past, those who defended their Church and through their faithfulness, living out the Gospel and teaching the Magisterium, led future generations to know and live a *Journey to Sainthood.* We need to know, so that we can read the road map, the Lord has laid out for us, the road to our Salvation and that of the world. Because the evil that man does, does live after him; but so does the good.

Our book is about the Cross, those who embraced it and lived their lives defending it. This book is about those who were born to defend not only the Church, but to embrace this Cross of Salvation, to willingly bear it when, like their Savior before them

---

[1]Luke 9:24

they were persecuted for speaking the Truth. It is about those Saints who discovered Jesus through His walk to Calvary and to the Cross. This book is about those who loved the Catholic Church which flowed from the Heart of Our Savior on that Cross, so passionately the enticements of this world faded into so much straw (St. Thomas Aquinas).

This book is about those who fought so that we would have a Church today, the battle between good and evil against untenable odds, and the Church was triumphant. Who will the Lord send today? Is it you, a member of your family, a friend, a fellow parishioner, a bishop, priest or religious you know? And what part will you have played? As we approach the Third Millennium, we feel the urgency with which Jesus walked the earth.

The time to act is now. We can make a difference! A little boy at Capharnaum brought up to Jesus what little he had, and Jesus blessed it, gave it to His disciples to distribute and they fed thousands of the children of God. This was with just five loaves and two fish? But it was Jesus' blessing that multiplied it to where, after feeding the multitudes there were twelve baskets full. What can you do? What part are you called to play? That of the little boy or have you been chosen to distribute the Word of God that has been blessed by Jesus, Who left its care in the hands of our first Pope and the first twelve apostles?

What can you do? St. Augustine said *"Tolle lege!"* Take and read about your family, the Saints who earned the titles in Heaven of *Defenders of the Faith*. Become a part of today's army of Defenders of the Faith which will usher the Church into the Third Millennium, victorious, triumphant!

Jesus loves you! Jesus needs you! Jesus wants you!

Saint Philip Neri
Apostle of the Laity

Coincidence; Holy Coincidence; or Holy Design that two Saints of the Counter-Reformation were *born* in the same year (1515) that Martin Luther began to espouse his theory on *Justification through Faith alone* and his criticism of Papal Indulgences which would culminate with the nailing of his controversial ninety-five theses on the doors of the Wittenburg Castle, two years later? As *one* of God's disciples is tripping and falling, God is sending down *two* disciples, one in Spain-Teresa of Avila and one in Italy-Philip Neri, to defend the Faith and counteract the misery which followed from this one act.

The Lord made a promise and He will not allow hell to prevail against His Church! During this dark period in the Church, Jesus had all sorts of future Saints balancing the scales; from Spain: Ignatius of Loyola, Teresa of Avila, John of the Cross; from Italy: Charles Borromeo, Philip Neri, Pius V, Robert Bellarmine, Catherine dei Ricci; from France: Vincent de Paul, Francis de Sales and Jane Frances de Chantal; from England: Thomas More and John Fisher. The Role Call of Defenders of the Faith goes on, with us just mentioning a few.

In the Garden of Eden, although God was sorrowful because the enemy had seduced his first human creatures, He immediately set a plan in motion for our Salvation, using His Son as the Spotless Lamb Who would redeem the world and a Spotless Vessel from which He would come into the world, our Mother Mary. The enemy, angry that God would send His Only Son to suffer and die for the very humans who would crucify Him, began unleashing his anger and hatred.

For two thousand years, the enemy has been doing everything in his power to destroy the Church.[1] And God has always raised powerful men and women, Defenders of the Faith

---

[1]Read more about heresies in Bob and Penny Lord's book: *Scandal of the Cross and Its Triumph, Heresies throughout the History of the Church.*

Above: *St. Philip Neri had a special love for Mother Mary.*

Above: *St. Philip Neri levitating while saying the Mass*

Above: *Death of St. Philip Neri*

Above: *St. Philip Neri at his deathbed*

Left: *Miracle of our Lady saving St. Philip Neri*

Above: *St. Philip Neri in Glory*

to counterbalance the enemy, or as in this period bring about a *Counter-Reformation.* In Europe, *6,000,000* Catholics were lost, as they were led, innocent lambs into a strange pasture; no more would they say the ancient prayers of their ancestors, attend the Sacrifice of the Mass or receive the Seven Sacraments. They didn't know they had been deceived into leaving their Church, until it was too late.

God, always true to His promise, balanced the books! He sent His Mother to the New World and the Church gained in less than seven years, 8,000,000 converts to the Catholic Church! Then why raise up these Saints? After all, the Church was well and alive; maybe not in Europe but in the New World. But as the Lord counts every hair on our heads,[2] and created each of us in His own Image, so precious is each soul to Him that He grieves at the loss of *one* of His lambs, and immediately summons a new army of shepherds to lead His lambs back to the pasture.[3]

The Church has been attacked and is wounded! From where will God call His next warrior?

[Bob and I say that one day, a light will rise in California that the whole country cannot fail to see, no less the world. It has to come from California, because this beautiful land, blessed by Junípero Serra and the first missionaries, has in many instances done so much harm. Not only shall this come to pass in this state; but a renewal has begun in this country, consecrated to the Blessed Mother, and our land will take her rightful place in the world as she was founded to be, *"a nation under God."*]

Why do we speak of this in connection with a Saint from a land across the sea, in a time almost five hundred years past? Because sadly and joyfully, history repeats itself. Whenever I look at the world at different periods of time, and how the Church and her children not only survived but triumphed, I have hope for our Church, for our country, for the world. But then as now God called forth *Defenders of the Faith* and they said Yes!

---

[2]*cf*Luke 21:18
[3]Catholic Church

A child is born who will be an instrument of love and peace

The world is in a mess, but no one knows it. Oh, there are a few voices in the wind, but everyone is too busy living the *Dolce Vita* to heed their pleas, no less convert and go back to God. Bath houses and revelry took the place of churches and reverence. They called it the Renaissance; today we have all sorts of names for those who even need justification to destroy all we have held dear - New Age is one; the One World Order is another. Then as now, the going philosophy was: There was no sin and only those who couldn't afford sin were against it. But God loves to raise soldiers who will fight, purposely choosing contradictions in the world, to confound the enemy. To make a fool out of the devil, God raised a young noble from the land of the Renaissance and called him to Sainthood.

The Good News is that the devil always goes too far, as with today, and people suddenly wake up, recognize who it is, and what it is he is doing, and they react! The only ever present danger that lies ahead with this turn-about-face is, if the faithful are not careful they will follow someone who sounds good, with the best of intentions, but who will lead them none-the-less far afield from the road to the Kingdom.

The Sixteenth Century was such a time; with no easy answers or quick fixes. Preachers were stemming from every hamlet, small and large, calling people to repent! And that was good, but they did it at the cost of unity and peace, supplanting the decadent past with a divided future. The Renaissance brought about a Luther and a Calvin, the pendulum swinging from the extreme left, to what was being touted as the extreme right. One of the big problems was that everyone became a lone ranger, teaching his own brand of religion.

What will stem the tide of promiscuity that threatens to flood Rome and then all of the papal states? Place an apostle right smack into the womb of the Renaissance. So, in the year 1515, as a raging storm ushered in a loud tempest of dissent in the north,[4] in the proud city of Florence a soft breeze, carrying the hope of the Church, introduced Philip Neri, future Saint and Apostle of Rome. God planted this true contradiction in his time, the Province of Tuscany, a land of the proud, willful and insolent, to a family of the nobility, who although righteous and good, were far from spiritual; their god, as with the rest of the aristocracy, was the god of convenience and luxury. His father and Philip's mother were born with a *golden* spoon in their mouths, from two of the wealthiest families in Tuscany.

From the time he was five years old, *"Pippo Buono"* ("good little Phil") was obedient, never willfully causing his parents any problems. But even Philip had his moments. One day, as he was praying the Psalter,[5] with one sister, another sister began teasing, trying to distract them. As words would not dissuade him, he gently pushed her away. Hearing the sister cry, little Phil's father scolded him. Phil was so remorseful, he cried, begging God to rid him of his lack of patience.

As he became known, people seeing him frequent the churches, and how kind and considerate he was of everyone, rich or poor, good *little* Phil became *good* Phil. His beloved mother died when Phil was very young, but the Lord sent him a very loving step-mother to care for him and his sisters. Phil's life of holiness, visiting the churches, praying the Psalms and etc. was to be interrupted when he reached eighteen years of age. It was time for him to prepare for his career; after all, born into such a family had its responsibilities. It was decided that Phil would go to his uncle. His uncle not only wanted to train him in the ways of commerce, he wished to leave his highly lucrative business to Phil when he died.

Always obedient, Phil left for Germano (near Monte Cassino). After arriving, he soon realized his old life was over. He missed home and the time he had to meditate on the Lord and His Passion. There was little time and less opportunity for

---

[4]Germany
[5]the book of Psalms

prayer. But Phil would finish his studies quickly and run off to a mountain near Monte Cassino called *"Split Mountain."* He would go there to pray and attend Mass. In the Shrine there was, in addition to the crucifix before which he prayed, a beautiful statue of the Blessed Mother. She appeared to him one day, told him he was to go to Rome, and his vocation was sealed!

A new life!

Without money, with only the clothes on his back, but with his uncle's and parents' reluctant blessing, a tired Phil arrived in Rome. An Archduke and friend of the family, who was also from Florence, engaged Phil to tutor his children. He lived a modest, austere life, in a room in the attic with a bed and a small table, eating a little bread and a few olives and sometimes some vegetables. With his loving example he converted the boys in his charge, from mischievous and self-willed, to holy young men who would go down into the catacombs with Phil to pray.

He wasted little time on frivolous matters, saying that fifteen minutes a day wasted on things that were not of God would add up to a considerable measure of time lost preparing for the most important thing that lay ahead - eternal life! He said, and I believe we will agree, that after spending time with people or things not relating to the spiritual life he came back to his quarters unsettled and disturbed, aching for the time missed getting closer to God. He said that he would notice, when he was with those of the world, his prayer life was affected; he was infected by the enemy's contagious virus of pride, vanity and love of things of the world.

Needless to say, the devil was interested in him. He sent young men to Phil who proceeded to share tales of their lewd behavior and desires. Rather than turn angrily on them, he spoke compassionately and lovingly of the Lord Who is so wounded by the lack of chastity; his tone so gentle they were remorseful and converted. But the devil never sleeps; when he could not tempt

Phil, as he was battling temptation with prayer, the *slimy one*[6] beat him mercilessly. This went on for the first fifty years of Philip Neri's life; mercifully God relieved him from the assaults of His enemy, his last thirty years. As he told his dear and trusted friend Cardinal Baronius, he grieved because he had not thanked God enough for the plentiful graces bestowed on him.

He practiced acts of mortification, saying that *little acts* of self-denial would help us combat *great attacks* waged against us by the enemy. Explaining he desired a true life of poverty like that of the Savior, he accepted none of his father's offers of assistance. Philip spent little or no time participating in the social life of Rome, but used every free moment when he was not praying or tutoring visiting the infirmed in hospitals. Each day, he tried to visit some or all the seven churches of Rome,[7] *St. Peter's Basilica, St. John Lateran,[8] St. Mary Major,[9] Scala Santa,[10] St. Paul outside the Walls,[11] St. Sebastian, St. Lawrence, and the Church of the Holy Cross of Jerusalem.* He often spent hours praying outside of locked churches, deep into the night, kneeling on the stone steps; or in the catacombs.

While praying in the Catacombs of St. Sebastian, the evening of the vigil of Pentecost, as Philip prayed for the Holy Spirit to descend upon him and fill him with His Spirit, he received the Holy Spirit in the form of huge ball of fire, soaring toward him. The ball of fire entered his mouth, traveled down to his heart, and finally rested there for the rest of his life. His heart was so on fire, he was filled with such passion, such ecstasy, he pleaded, *"Stop Lord! I cannot take anymore. Anymore and I*

---

[6]what a holy priest, Father Pablo Straub calls Satan
[7]most frequented by pilgrims
[8]This is the Cathedral of Rome, and as Bishop of Rome, the Pope's church; not St. Peter's Basilica
[9]the oldest church in Rome, dedicated to the Mother of God
[10]stairs Jesus ascended to be condemned to death by Pilate. St. Helena, Constantine's mother brought them to Rome from Jerusalem.
[11]where St. Paul died and is buried

will die!" This fire would remain with him the rest of his days, from age twenty to eighty, sixty years! His heart became so enlarged, as a result his two ribs broke. When he meditated on the Lord and His Sacrifice for us, his heart would beat so loudly, it sounded like the rumbling of an earthquake; for this reason, they dubbed him *Saint of the Earthquake.* They said that it could be heard all the way to St. Peter's, about two miles away.

He had a deep devotion to Jesus Crucified. As a young man he could not pray in front of Jesus hanging on the Crucifix before him, without grieving passionately, as if he were there at Golgotha and Jesus was breathing His last.

Philip was a brilliant student and delved deeply into theology and the writings of the early Church fathers, Holy Scripture, and the Canons of the Church. He treasured this knowledge. He learned early that you cannot love that which you do not know and cannot teach that which you do not love; if you do not teach with love and knowledge you are just tossing words around which will soon be forgotten; without love and passion, it means nothing to the student and he does not learn; equal to the passion you show will be the passion the student will have toward the subject.

St. Philip Neri was an outstanding scholar, renowned for his knowledge of the Faith; but at twenty years of age, seeing the plight of the poor, he sold his precious books to supply what money he could to feed them and make their life easier. He was so in love with this God become Man that he would plead at times, *"Depart from me, Oh Lord; Depart from me! I am a mere mortal, and I am not able to bear such overwhelming joy and ecstasy."* And then at other times, he was overheard saying, *"O, God, seeing You are so lovable, how come You only gave us but one heart to love You, and it so narrow and little."* His biographers say if the Lord had not lessened His love at these times, Philip Neri would have prematurely died from ecstasy!

Those who knew him best, his first biographers, Cardinal Baronius and Galloni, said that the heart was so affected by *good*

Phil's ecstasies, the third and fourth ribs on the left side broke to accommodate the size of the heart enlarging and decreasing with each ecstasy. Not only this but the ribs had to make room for the aftermath, resulting from the acute thumping, pounding, throbbing, palpitations of the heart and the effect it had on the other organs in his chest. [All this phenomenon was affirmed by doctors and members of the Church after Philip Neri died.]

Apostle of the Laity, Philip begins to evangelize

Being of the Laity and never feeling worthy to be a priest, Philip Neri desired nothing but to serve as a lay man. He had been preaching in the hospitals, then on the street corners waiting for the office workers to leave for lunch or home. He would speak to them, instruct them with the true teachings of the Church. He taught with such love, such fire that more and more came, and stayed longer and longer, until they began following him, visiting the poor and the infirmed; and the Confraternity of the Laity was formed! The Confraternity was not only filled with these young people, now on fire for the Faith, but with the nobility.

The Apostolate took on the care of poor pilgrims coming to Rome for the Holy Year. Since most of them arrived sick, tired, without much to eat, having walked hundreds of miles under the worst conditions, they had need not only of a place to stay, but often a hospital. St. Philip and his Confraternity set up the first pilgrims' houses in Rome, where they could stay a short time, convalesce or receive more intensive hospital care.

The time came for Philip Neri to become *Father* Philip Neri. His confessor convinced him he could do more good fighting the heresies and paganism destroying the very fiber of our Church and the Mystical Body of Christ, as a priest. He obeyed! He was ordained at thirty-six. His first Mass, he became so overcome with emotion, shaking almost uncontrollably, he could barely pour the wine and water into the chalice. At the moment of Consecration, when he elevated the Host, he had to lean against the altar for support, as he feared he would fall over if he did not brace himself. This would repeat itself at every Mass he said.

He was never too sick to celebrate the ongoing *Sacrifice of the Cross every day.* He united himself so deeply with the Lord, His last hours on the Cross, that at the moment of elevation, he would levitate, suspended over the altar for more than two hours. For this reason, toward the end of his life, in order to not attract attention to himself, rather than to the Mass and what is truly happening on the altar, he celebrated Mass privately in a little chapel adjacent to his room. His first biographer said he came upon St. Philip many times, elevated as high as six feet from the floor while saying the Mass.

One day, during the celebration of the Sacrifice of the Mass, as he was supplicating Jesus to give him the gift of patience, he heard an inner voice say, *"You'll have it; the road to Heaven is through the Cross."* The Lord was to soon show him the meaning behind his words! Father Philip Neri went to live in the Church of San Geròlamo[12] where he was persecuted by two bishops who inflicted the cruelest insults upon him, accusing him of deserting his family and the responsibilities connected with his former title and birthright. He bore it all with humility and patience.

He continued to preach, but now not only from the pulpit but from the confessional. During the forty hour devotions, which he loved, he preached so passionately about the God-Man Jesus Who was alive in the Monstrance that one day there were thirty conversions, young men who had come to church to ridicule Father Neri and disrupt the Mass, but after hearing him, converted and asked to go to confession. More and more people returned to the Sacraments after many years away from the Church. He began teaching in his private chamber; from this, more and more came, and before you know it the Congregation

---

[12]Italian for St. Jerome

of the Oratory was formed. Philip Neri was thirty seven years old.

The Church is under siege, and the heretics are attacking the very lifeline of the Church, the **Sacraments**. How does St. Philip Neri respond to this abuse? He begins to preach on the necessity of receiving the Sacraments: The Sacrament of *Baptism* soon after the birth of a child; The Sacrament of *Confirmation*, the final initiation into the Church - the Sacrament which calls us to become *Soldiers of Christ*; The Sacrament of *Extreme Unction*,[13] the merciful *last kiss* of the Church; The Sacraments of *Reconciliation* and *Holy Communion* and the need of frequent reception of these Sacraments to be strong; the awesome sanctity of The Sacrament of *Holy Orders*; and the sacred union between husband and wife and Jesus the day they are united under the *Sacrament of Matrimony*.

His sermons attracted so many to the Sacraments, he often had to hear confessions into the wee hours of the night, sometimes ending with the rising of the morning sun. But he was so happy! Never too tired, he would wash his face, maybe catch a couple of hours of sleep and off he would go to the confessional to hear more hearts cleansed of their sins returning to Jesus. Philip Neri had all the gifts; one of which was the ability to read men's hearts. When a penitent needed help making a good examination of conscience, and was struggling during confession, Philip Neri would reveal the penitent's most hidden, innermost sins, and with that helped the penitent to make a good confession.

Philip Neri heard the call to go to India as a missionary. He immediately asked to go. The answer was: *"Your India is Rome; it is to the Romans you are to bring the Word of God."* Although disappointed, he obeyed!

Philip Neri went after heretics with love but also firmness. No heretic was safe around him; the hardest hearts were softened

---

[13]Last Rights or Sacrament of the Sick

and accepted Mother Church as the one True Church. There was a heretic who was awaiting being burned at the stake, as this was the punishment for heresy by the state, at this time. Nothing or no one could persuade him to renounce his errors and ask pardon of Mother Church. He obstinately refused all pleas made to him to save his life and immortal soul. He would hear nothing of it. Enter St. Philip! After he spoke to him gently and lovingly, the heretic repented, retracted publicly his errors and asked pardon of the Church; as a consequence he was saved from death.

Saint Philip Neri goes after the devil and his works

St. Philip Neri expelled demons! As Persiano Rosa, his confessor was dying, he was attacked by the devil who appeared in the form of a black dog. As soon as Philip Neri entered the room, Rosa asked him to pray for him. No sooner had Philip Neri knelt and begun praying, than the prince of hell fled, howling in anger and mortification.

The Carnival and its perversion enveloped and swallowed much of Rome's society, the rich and the poor united in its debauchery. Philip Neri came up with a solution: He instituted the visitation of the seven churches of Rome, to be done during the Carnival. First members of the Confraternity processed; then others joined, first out of curiosity and then desire. As holiness is eternally *beautiful*, and evil everlastingly *ugly*, the young, tired of the depravity of the Carnival, were attracted by the solemnity of the procession and processors; soon more and more joined the *holy parade* to the seven churches.

Like Jesus, Father Philip Neri was always calling God's creatures to be as He had designed them to be, not as the world had refashioned them. He asked Fiora[14] and some other penitents to take in orphans, clean them up, feed them and teach them how to live holy lives in the world.

Charity toward all, his heart bled most for the poor and the sick. One day, as he and one of his Confraternity were passing

---

[14]means flower in Italian

by the Coliseum, he came upon a person lying in the street, more dead than alive. The man called out, *"Do I revolt you?"* Father Philip Neri's response was to ask his spiritual son to lift the man and bring him to their hospital.[15]

Our Lady comes to the rescue!

Mother Mary was always there for Philip Neri, as she is for us, whether we love her, believe in her Immaculate Conception, or accept her as the Mother of God; she is always waiting, ready to help us. Once when Philip was laying in bed, so ill they judged he would not last the night, Our Lady appeared to him. He was so overwhelmed by her radiant beauty, he fell into a rapture and cried out, *"O most holy Mother of God, what have I done that you should vouchsafe[16] to come to me?"* She would always come to him, in time of need, like her Son, guarding every hair on his head.

Father Philip Neri was given an old church, *Santa Maria in Vallicella*, for his Confraternity to live and work in. Now, the enemy was upset, as he was aware of all the good that would come about in this, God's house. The building was in need of renovation, so Father and all his companions began at once to ready it for the Lord, Who would dwell in the Tabernacle and come to life in all the Masses that would be celebrated there. There was much joy and excitement, everyone making plans; meanwhile catastrophe was lurking in the shadows, waiting to strike. Father was supervising the repairs of the old church, when a cross beam[17] supporting the roof became loose. It was about to crash down on Father Neri, when who should appear, but the Virgin Mary. His Heavenly Mother put up her arms and held the beam upright, balancing it, until someone took it from her.[18]

---

[15]the one they had set up for just this purpose
[16]be gracious enough
[17]a 6"x12" beam running the length of the church
[18]This was testified by those who were present at the time.

As she had done in the past, she was just watching over her children, those whom Jesus had given Her at the foot of the Cross. And she was saying with this action, *"Be not afraid, I will continue to do so."* She was showing Father Philip Neri that she would always be there, protecting him and all his spiritual sons and daughters from harm.

Saint Philip has the gift of Prophecy

Philip Neri meets Francis de Sales and predicts his future. Philip Neri first met Francis de Sales when Francis was still young and Philip had just a few years to live. Saint to Saint, the older priest looked into the young graduate's[19] eyes, embraced him and predicted he would one day earn a reputation as a brilliant scholar and Defender of the Faith. Years later, when Philip encountered Francis, as Archbishop of Geneva, he was already famous and highly respected. At this time, Philip Neri prophesied that Francis de Sales would become known as *"the pious, sweet tamer of Heretics;"* and as such would suffer much; but that he would accomplish great feats for Mother Church. Then he revealed circumstances as yet unknown to Francis. Having finished, the loving Neri embraced Francis, the younger soldier and defender of Christ and His Church, and bid him farewell. Philip Neri would, in just a few years, be praying for Francis de Sales before the Throne of God.

St. Philip Neri prophesied for Cardinals and Popes; he told Cardinal Nicole that he would be elected Pope, and later as Pope Gregory XIV he showed his respect for Philip Neri by kissing the feet of his prophet, much to St. Neri's uneasiness, in front of the entire Curia. Pope Gregory, with profound respect for Philip Neri offered him the red cap of a Cardinal. St. Philip respectfully refused, pleading his unworthiness. This was to be just one persecution, as laughter and derision filled the room, from the Cardinals!

---

[19]he had just graduated from the University of Padua

Philip Neri was Camillus de Lellis's confessor, and the young future Saint relied heavily on his advice. Only after he received permission, would Camillus seek to be ordained. He began his priesthood in the Church of San Giacomo, but then began his own Order called *Priests of the Sick.* Always judging himself, the worst of sinners, he was *again* confessing his unworthiness, when St. Philip reassured him of his holiness and that of his Order by sharing how many times, he had seen Angels hovering over Camillus' priests as they were ministering to the dying, whispering the right words to say.

Cardinals wrote about Philip Neri during his lifetime, this is why we have so much information on this powerful Saint. Of his hand, there is nothing, as before he died, he burned all his brilliant poetry and writings.   Had he not done this, out of humility, or had he had a community like St. Teresa of Avila, who without her knowledge copied her writings (or the world would not have hers either, as she obeyed the Inquisition and burned all her writings), he would have most assuredly been proclaimed *Doctor of the Church.*

Saint Philip Neri, model of purity

God protected him, always!   He gave him the gift to discern good from evil.   The odor of sanctity was a sweet perfume to Philip; whereas the stench of impurity was so putrid, it would pierce his being, penetrate his nostrils like an invasive burning acid, travel down into his throat, scorching his insides with the most excruciating fire.   One day, he was passing by some young ladies of the Court, resplendently attired, but not even the fine, exotic perfumes could hide the horrendous stench of impurity that emanated from them.   He was forced to cover his nose, till he was a great distance, or risk becoming ill.   From this incident, he taught that we either flee from impurity or the impure flame will burn wildly out of control, and corrupt our very hearts.

When you hold up the mirror of piety to one who is sinning, it reflects so powerfully the contrast to the sinner's life, he either converts, or tries to break the mirror.   One night, upon entering his chamber, he was greeted by two women of the night with unsavory reputations, who had been planted there to seduce him. He looked at them; they could not be over sixteen years old. He began to cry, weeping profusely over their loss of innocence and, rather than condemn them, spoke to them of Jesus and Mary Magdalene. They knelt at his feet and asked him for forgiveness. The next day, they went to confession and returned to the Sacraments, a new life before them.

He always imparted the need to have good and holy companions. He would often lead the children in his care, to a safe place where they could play free from the corrupt influence of children who were always up to some kind of mischief, more often than not, ending with grave repercussions. After St. Philip started them off playing innocent games, he would go rest under a tree and pray for the safekeeping of their immortal souls; his advice, *"Play pure games and remain happy. Stay far away from the worldly who have perilous dangers ready, to share with you."*

The devil never left *good Phil* alone, trying endlessly to fill his head with *"little nothing temptations."* But St. Philip knew there was no such thing as *little temptations*, as little temptations, like little sins, lead to serious sin. One day when the enemy was attacking him, filling his head with all sorts of temptations, such as inducing his senses to rebel, Philip began to pray fervently and flagellate himself; in this way he overcame the devil, foiling his attempts to use the flesh against the spirit. Drained, drenched with sweat pouring from the onslaught, he was in peace. He never forgot that *"only in God will we find our much needed peace."*

Saint Philip Neri is seen levitating

The Saints have to work at remaining pure; *purity* is not a gift one receives and can afford to neglect. Even a Saint, like Philip Neri fought temptations of one kind or another, the enemy of God always trying to snare the *unsnarable*.[20] One time when St. Philip Neri was seriously ill, Francesco, one of his spiritual children, entered the room, and saw St. Philip *levitating*, suspended over his bed in ecstasy, thanking the Lord for having rescued him from a serious temptation.[21]

Miracles abound while St. Philip is still alive.

He bi-located! A young man was drowning, when suddenly St. Philip appeared; lifting him up out of the sea, he pulled him to shore.

He performed a triple miracle. In another instance, St. Philip predicted that three young man would go to Corsica, would drown in the middle of the sea, and end up in Rome, where they would be raised from the dead. All this came to pass, when St. Philip Neri was still alive.

He liberated those possessed by the devil. One day, he was called to exorcise a demon from Catherine d'Aversa; as he was praying over her, a demon resembling a mad dog came out of her and flew toward him. Philip took a mace and flung it wildly at the demon and he disappeared.

There was a young man who was possessed. St. Philip Neri entered the room and addressed the demon demanding, *"Do you know who I am?"* Taken aback by his holiness and strength, and fearing his authority, the demon came out of the youth in a cloud of gray smoke!

St. Philip had been confessor to a young prince who was now on his death bed. He asked the youth, if he wanted to get well; to which he answered, *"I want the Will of God."*

The young prince was now dying, and he called for St. Philip. He couldn't go because he was celebrating Mass, and the young prince died. After the Mass was over, St. Philip ran immediately to the palace. The royal family was gathered around the prince's bed, grieving. When St. Philip learned that the youth

---

[20]Author takes poetic liberty here, substituting for unattainable
[21]It is not written what the temptation could have been.

had wanted to confess once more before dying, he began to weep. Then he blessed the prince with Holy Water. He put a little of the water on the prince's lips, placed his hand on him, and called out, *"Paul! Paul!"*

The youth opened his eyes and filled with joy, he said, *"Father, how much I prayed for you to come. I had forgotten a sin and I wanted to confess."*[22] The saint told everyone to leave the room and after hearing his confession, St. Philip asked the youth, *"Are you now content to die?"* At which he answered, *"Yes Father, because now I know I am going to Heaven."* St. Philip said *"I bless you. Go in peace."* The little prince died, his eyes filled with peace as he gave up his spirit.

Great personages came to Saint Philip Neri

He was honored and sought after by Kings and Queens, even by Popes, Pius IV, Pius V, Gregory XIII, Gregory XIV, and Clement VIII. One Pope held him in such high esteem, that at an audience, he bent over to St. Philip Neri who was kneeling before him, and reverently kissed his hand. St. Philip humbly accepted this show of love from his pontiff.

Greats in the Church and powerful movers and shakers of the Counter-Reformation came to Philip Neri, for advice, like St. Vincent de Paul who used St. Neri's Oratory as a model for his Oratory. The most highly respected minds in the Church turned to him, including *St. Charles Borromeo*, who venerated St. Philip Neri as a Saint while he was still alive, *St. Ignatius of Loyola*, who saw a ball of fire over the Church of San Girolamo where St. Philip Neri was staying (and St. Philip Neri saw a halo of light around the head of St. Ignatius of Loyola).

Time for our Saint to go Home; and we and his Order grieve

April was hard on Philip Neri with him in bed, the whole month, his body burning with fever! May came and with it, fever, frequent bouts of vomiting and massive hemorrhaging. It was time! Caesar Baronius gave our tired Saint *Extreme Unction*

---

[22]Everyone there witnessed this miracle.

and the hemorrhaging stopped. Then Cardinal Frederick
Borromeo came with the Viaticum and with the amazement of
those grieving by his bedside, Philip Neri sat up, tears spilling
down his cheeks, and exclaimed in a loud, clear voice, *"Behold
my love, my Love! He comes, the only delight of my soul! Give
me my Love quickly!"*

He turned to His Lord before him in the Sacred Host, *"I
was never worthy of receiving Thy Body; nor have I done any
good."* Then after he received his final Holy Communion, he
sighed, *"I have received the Physician in my lodging."*

Many Masses had been said for him and he seemed to be
rallying. That day, he heard confessions as usual and appeared
healthier than he had in years. But he had foretold that this was
the day of his death,[23] and he counted the hours, in excited
anticipation of that moment when at last his eyes would feast on
the Beatific Vision of Our Lord and his soul at last rest in the
arms of His Blessed Mother.

It was just minutes after midnight. That day they had
celebrated the Feast of Corpus Christi, May 26th. Forever the
priest, having had the gift of celebrating one last time, the Mass
of that glorious Feast Day honoring His Savior, in the Holy
Eucharist, the valiant Defender of the Church, who lived every
moment for her, loving her, serving her, defending her, extolling
her merits and gifts more by *who* he was then by *what* he said,
went Home.

Miracles began immediately, while he was laid out, the
walls at his shrine covered with ex-votos showing thousands of
miracles brought about through his intercession. Seven years
after his death, a splendid chapel was built to house the tomb of
our humble Saint. When they exhumed the body they found it to
be completely incorrupt.

In 1622, twenty-seven years after his death, Pope Gregory
XV canonized our Saint.

---

[23]as many later testified

Above: *Saint Francis de Sales was born in this castle near Annecy, France.*

Right: *Saint Francis de Sales being ordained Bishop of Geneva.*

Above:
Saint Francis de Sales Defender of the Faith Founder of the Visitation Order, Doctor of the Church, Patron of Journalists Apostle of the Chablais

Below:
Annecy, France House of Savoy, Chateau de Thuille home of St. Francis de Sales

Left: *Saint Francis de Sales and St. Jane Frances de Chantal are buried here in the Church of the Visitation in Annecy, France.*

St. Francis de Sales

"The measure of love is to love without measure."

Whenever the Church is threatened, the Lord raises up a Saint or two or brings about Miracles. In this instance, the Lord raised up two Saints, St. Francis de Sales, the Bishop of Geneva, a Doctor of the Church, and Founder of a Religious Order and St. Jane Frances de Chantal. He also gave us many Miracles, including the softening of men's hearts.

The years 1567 through 1622 were not great years for Catholics in Switzerland. They were not especially good years for a bishop of the Catholic Church, in particular the Bishop of Geneva. For that task, the Lord had to search all over Heaven until He could find a special soul who would not only be *capable* of pastoring the people of God during the period of hell caused by John Calvin, but would be *willing* to take on the job. The soul who would be Francis de Sales was the perfect candidate. So the Lord blessed him, gave him special Angels to guide and protect him, covered him in the mantle of Mother Mary, and sent him on his way. He was to be the first of thirteen babies the Lord would give to this special family. But of all, this was the prize, given from the Lord.

The Angels delivered the future St. Francis de Sales to a beautiful château in what was called Thorens at that time, but today is just outside the breathtakingly city of Annecy, France, on Lake Geneva. He was born in a château on August 21, 1567. His family was part of the House of Savoie, which was a noble family in Europe. On the following day St. Francis was baptized in the Parish church of Thorens, and given the name *Francis Bonaventure*. His patron saint was the Little Poverello of Assisi.[1] He was named after St. Francis and Bonaventure, another famous Franciscan and Doctor of the Church. [St. Bonaventure, *Seraphic Doctor*, was born just five years before

---

[1]St. Francis

St. Francis died, and followed in the Poverello's footsteps.] The combination of qualities exemplified in Francis, who was all heart, and in Bonaventure, who was brilliant, were just the traits young Francis would need in his ministry for the Church, as he grew in body and spirit.

What were his parents thinking about for this, their first baby? Would he continue in the House of Savoie, taking care of the land, his heritage? Would Francis Bonaventure follow in the footsteps of his namesakes? Although we read that both parents were traditional Catholics, could they have had any idea what they were doing when they gave such powerful names to their newborn? Nothing is by coincidence, not even the naming of a child. Unless it is *God's Holy Coincidence*.

The room in which he was born was known as St. Francis' room, because of a painting in the room of the Saint preaching to the birds and the fishes. It was always young Francis' favorite painting of his namesake, as was this his favorite room.

Francis was born prematurely, leaving him frail and delicate, physically challenged as a young child. But he was never *Spiritually* challenged. From his earliest childhood, he was unusually active and energetic. He was a product of Home Schooling in his early years. His mother kept his education in her own hands, aided by a tutor, Abbé Déage, a local priest who was very learned. As Francis grew, this priest became his tutor, traveling with him everywhere during his youth. Beautiful traits were instilled in him by the Lord, who guided his mother in his upbringing his entire life. He was obedient and truthful no matter what the consequences. In addition, he was a voracious reader; he devoured every book he could get. He was very eager to learn. The Lord was gearing him up for a mighty job and he couldn't begin too soon.

In the year 1575, Francis, now eight years old, attended the college of Annecy, which was just a few miles distance from the château. There, he was prepared for First Holy Communion and Confirmation. He received both Sacraments on the same day, December 17, 1577 at the tender age of ten years old in the local church in Annecy. It was the most important day of his life, one which he would never forget. In September of the following year, he received the tonsure. Tonsure at that time, was the introductory ceremony by which a layman became a cleric. It was not part of the Sacrament of Holy Orders, but was sort of the initiation process. [There are different ways to receive tonsure. One is cutting small portions from the front, back, two sides and the crown of the head. Another method is to shave the top of the head in a circle, leaving just a crown of hair as a permanent tonsure.]

Now, under normal circumstances, this would be considered unusual, because to the best of our knowledge, tonsure is only given to someone who is in a religious order. In the time of St. Francis de Sales, tonsure was allowed even if the candidate had no intention of taking the Sacrament of Holy Orders. However, years later, Francis confided to his father that he had always had a great wish to consecrate himself to God and he regarded this as the first bold step. His father had other plans for him, which did not include the religious life in any way, and so he didn't take seriously, his son's desire for the religious life.

In 1581, at fourteen years old, Francis was sent to the University of Paris, which at that time was among the top centers of learning in Europe. His father's agenda called for Francis to enter the Collège de Navarre, as it was frequented by the sons of the noble families of Savoie. The courses offered there would be perfect for the life Monsieur Boisy[2] had envisioned for Francis, of which he made no secret. But Francis, who had kept his feelings about what he wanted to do with his life, to himself, feared the influence this school would have on his commitment to

---

[2]Boisy - name taken by Francis' father upon marrying his mother, who was nobility. She was of the House of Savoie - he was not. However, Francis' name remained De Sales.

the Lord, and preferred to be allowed to go to the Collège de Clermont, which was under Jesuit direction, and renowned for piety as well as for learning. In this college, he would be able to study rhetoric, philosophy and theology under the supervision of the Jesuits. He was able to get his father to agree, which was a miracle in itself. So he and his tutor, Abbé Déage, took up residence in a hotel near the Collège de Clermont, and he embarked on the greatest adventure of his life. He excelled in the atmosphere of spiritual teaching, but in addition, and very astutely, in order to please his father, he took lessons in noble endeavors, riding, dancing and fencing.

Those six years in Paris were very important in his formation. He was able to accomplish both tasks. He gave to God the things that were God's; he gave to Caesar the things that were Caesar's. He became a man of the Renaissance, (the good part of the Renaissance, if that's possible), obtaining a bachelor of art's degree. But he also studied Theology and Scripture. Spiritually, his life centered on meditation, devotion to the Eucharist and Our Lady.

His love was in treasures from above, not those of this world. His heart was more and more set upon giving himself wholly to God. He made a vow of *perpetual chastity* and placed himself under the special protection of our dear Mother Mary. He should have known when he did those two things, vowed chastity and placed himself under the mantle of Mary, that he was in trouble. As the Lord knew the powerful work Francis would do for the Kingdom and the people of Geneva and Savoie, the evil one knew as well.

The attacks began hot and heavy on Francis, when he reached eighteen years old. He was besieged by unbelievable, painful temptation to despair. His whole life had always revolved around his relationship with God; but suddenly he was victim of a dreaded apprehension that he had lost God, that His Grace was no longer flowing through him, and that he would spend his eternity condemned to hell, hating God, the torture of the accursed. For us, looking at what was happening in hindsight, it was as if he were experiencing the Dark Night of the Soul to which most Saints are subjected, at some time in their lives. But usually, it's a lot later in their walk with the Lord. Perhaps God wanted him to get it out of the way prior to beginning this lifelong mission in His Service.

It got so bad that it was affecting him physically. His health suffered intensely from the ongoing excruciating mental anguish. He tried to offer it up for the Poor Souls in Purgatory, to which he had a great devotion. But it didn't help. "*Lord*" he cried, "*if I'm ever to see Thee in Heaven, this at least, grant me that I may never curse nor blaspheme Thy Holy Name. If I may not love Thee in the other world, for in Hell, none praise Thee, let me at least, every instance of my brief existence here, love Thee as much as I can.*"[3]

But, in the midst of this torture, while praying the Memorare[4] to Our Lady for help, suddenly all anxiety suddenly left him. He could feel the mantle of Mary covering him. In his soul, he could hear the Angels singing songs of praise to God; a blanket of peace covered him. It was over. From this experience, he learned a number of important lessons early in his ministry. The first was to reach out to Mary immediately when he was in trouble. Another important point was to try to understand and deal tenderly with the spiritual difficulties and temptations of others.

When he returned home in 1588, after six years studying in Paris, his father wanted him to become involved in the service of the state, in keeping with his position as a member of the House of Savoie. He sent him to Padua to study Law at the University

---

[3]Butler's Lives of the Saints Vol I - Pg 196
[4]Read how the Memorare played an important part in the conversion of a Jewish man through the Miraculous Medal in Bob & Penny Lord's book, "*The Many Faces of Mary, a love story*"

of Padua, one of the greatest universities in Europe. But the Lord was not going to allow him to just waste time learning Law. In addition to taking his courses in secular Law, he took courses in Canon Law. Also, he was able to study more theology. The Lord then placed a Jesuit in his path, Anthony Possevin. Francis was very impressed with the spirituality of the man. He asked him to be his Spiritual Director. Through this experience, God was able to keep Francis focused on his real treasures while in the center of materialism and Renaissance. He had to keep his soul free from the enticements all around him. One of the greatest positives which came from his relationship with the Jesuit was that he drew up a personal rule for life, interior and exterior. He renewed his commitment to virginity and the Divine Office, which he had made in Paris some years before.

St. Francis was twenty four years old when he received his final degree and became a doctor of law at Padua. However, we have a slight hitch here. While he accomplished what his father had sent him to Padua for, the degree in civil Law, he also on his own received a degree in Canon Law. So he continued working for the Father, in preparation for whatever the Lord had planned for him.

Before going back to his family in Annecy, he made a pilgrimage to Rome, returning by way of Venice and Loreto in Italy. Whatever desires he had to turn his life over to the Lord were that much multiplied after having spent time where the roots of his Church, the roots of his life, lay. He spent a good deal of time in Rome, and then, on the way back home, decided he had to visit the holiest shrine to Our Lady in the world, the Holy House of Loreto.[5] To that end, he sailed up the Adriatic Sea to Ancona, and took a carriage to the shrine he had only read about. As he approached the great Basilica, which housed the Santa

---

[5]Read the entire account of the Holy House of Loreto, where the Angels brought the Holy House of Nazareth from Israel to the shores of Italy in 1294 in Bob and Penny Lord's book, *Heavenly Army of Angels*

Casa, the home of the Holy Family while they were in Nazareth, his heart beat so loudly, he thought he would burst.

He rushed to the little house inside the Basilica, and just stayed there, praying, looking at the image of Our Lady which had come with the house when the Angels brought it from the Holy Land to Italy by way of Tersatto, in Croatia. Tradition has it that the statue of Our Lady and the child Jesus was carved by the Evangelist St. Luke. Our young future Saint, Bishop and Doctor of the Church could not tear himself away from that little house, made into a chapel. He stayed there all day. He went into ecstasy for the first time in his life here at the shrine to the Holy Family. He cried during the time he was with her. We don't know what transpired. He never wrote about it. His companion, Abbé Déage, witnessed his ecstasy. As evening wore on, the setting sun cast long shadows down upon the interior of the shrine, and Francis hid in one of those precious shadows provided by brother sun. His heart beat so fast, he thought he would die. He had never done anything like this. He wanted to stay in the Church the entire evening. Finally, he saw the huge main door close, and heard the grinding of the keys against the metal of the door. It was closed. He was alone with Our Lady.

He prayed the whole night inside the Holy House. We don't know what might have happened in there. Did Our Lady come to him and share what his future life would be like? Did he receive consolation from the Angels when it became pitch dark, and the noises of the church frightened him? It is written there at the shrine that on the evening he spent at the Holy House, St. Francis de Sales made his own personal vow of chastity for life. It was given directly to the Heavenly Family by Our Lady of Loreto. She brought it to the Throne of her Son, who accepted it. Francis' life was sealed.

He went back to his family at the Château de Thuille on the lake of Annecy after his pilgrimage. He waited patiently for eighteen months, outwardly at least, leading what everyone considered the ordinary life of a young noble of his time. He reminds us somewhat of his namesake, Francis of Assisi, who returned from Spoleto after the wars and waited for the Lord to tell him what to do. There's a favorite poster of ours which shows St. Francis speaking to the Lord. He asks *"What do you want me to do?"*

Francis de Sales might very well have been doing the same. He was experiencing a certain amount of pressure from his father, which was normal. Remember, Francis hadn't told his father anything about his vocation. His father fully expected that Francis was going to go into a suitable business. After all, he had sent him to a college in Paris, and the University of Padua; he had a degree in law. On that course, his father procured him a highly esteemed post in the government, a senatorial seat, through the Duke of Savoy. His father also teamed him up with a very attractive, eligible young lady of the nobility, who would have made a perfect wife. The match would be good for both families. Francis declined both the dignity offered him of becoming a member of the senate of Savoie, which was an unusual honor for so young a man, and the opportunity to marry his father's choice. However, he did not explain why.

Francis had so far only told his mother, his cousin Louis de Sales, a priest and Canon in the church of Geneva and some other friends and relatives, how he wanted to give his life to the service of God. He had not confided to his father, and a confrontation would soon become unavoidable. His father was greatly chagrined by his son's refusal of the position of senator, and his determination not to marry. But none of these disappointments appeared to have prepared him for the blow of Francis' vocation. Francis attempted to get his old tutor, Abbé Déage, to gently break the news to his father. But the old friend refused. Francis then turned to his cousin, Canon Louis de Sales. His cousin told him that possibly the Lord might have brought this to a head at the perfect moment.

The death of the provost[6] of the chapter of Geneva suggested the possibility that Francis might be appointed to this post. This could possibly soften the blow to his father of knowing what his son wanted to do with his life. Everybody seemed to be willing to take part in this plot. They even received help from the Bishop of Geneva.

When the cousin had suggested submitting Francis for the appointment, Francis didn't take it too seriously, not giving it much hope; so without consulting any of the family, his cousin applied to the Pope, with whom the appointment rested, and the letters instituting Francis as Provost of the chapter were promptly received from Rome.

When the appointment was announced to Francis, he almost collapsed. He didn't for a moment think he was capable of handling the job, but then he remembered his time with Our Lady in the Holy House. With a great deal of reluctance he accepted the honor. He prayed that somehow this might turn his father's anger to love and softness, and he would allow his son to have the life he really wanted.

There were a few reasons why the father did not want to give in to this request. First off, Francis was the eldest of thirteen children. He could just imagine having to go through this with all of them. He truly believed, and it was rather standard at that time, that children regard the wishes of the father as the final word on a subject. *Secondly*, he was the oldest; his father had sort of planned out the lives of all his children, and they all meshed in together. One of them breaking the mold could really create a problem, possibly interfering with his plan for them; and if that someone is the firstborn, well.... In addition, he loved this boy very much. He did not want anything to happen to him. Being a Catholic priest in this section of France, and connected

---

[6]Provost - the head of a Cathedral Chapter or Church - not necessarily a priest, but preferable

to the Diocese of Geneva, was tantamount to asking for a death sentence. Many years before, Calvin had come into the city of Geneva, and used it to make a perfect Calvinist city. He aided the people in banishing both the Duke of Savoie, and the Bishop of Geneva, who had gone to Annecy, which is where Francis had met him.

There were many tales of persecution and execution of whoever Calvin considered to be heretics, and he considered most Catholics to be heretics. He ran an occupied country, in which everyone had to adhere to his rules. Attendance of the Calvinist Church was mandatory; those disobeying were subject to punishment and risked being put to the rack; and anyone preaching against the Calvinist party line was executed. The rank and file people could not understand how this had happened to them in just fifty or seventy five years, but they were living in a topsy-turvy world where everything which had been illegal was now not only legal, but the law of the land. What had been heresy was now gospel. This is the life that Canon Louis de Sales and Francis de Sales were recommending for Francis to his father. It required all the patient persuasion, prayers and novenas before his father finally gave his consent. Then he began to pray the Rosary often and make many novenas for his son's welfare.

Francis was not about to take any chances. He immediately began wearing clerical garb, and six months afterwards, on December 18, 1593, he was ordained a priest. While it was just the beginning, he envisioned doing great work for the Lord. He began working immediately with the poor and homeless, the sick and addicted. He spent much time in the confessional, bringing back those who had left. There were many apostates who wanted to come back to the Church. He had to welcome them in the name of those who had suffered and seen family members tortured and killed because they would not give up the Faith. So in those instances, he not only had to bring back the apostate, he had to ask forgiveness from those who wanted to kill the apostate. His work was truly cut out for him.

He did a great deal of preaching. At the beginning, he confined himself to Annecy, but as he developed more confidence, and was more accepted, he spread out to areas outside Annecy. But he didn't venture into any dangerous areas....yet! He was being prepared by the Lord, however to evangelize in the dangerous areas around Lake Geneva.

This area, the Chablais, which had been ruled by the House of Savoie, had been invaded sixty years before by militant Protestants from Berne who took over the western part of it as well as some provinces on the north shore of the lake. Catholic worship was outlawed, and churches were burned or destroyed when not appropriated for Protestant use. Religious orders were suppressed and priests were exiled.

Thirty years later, the Duke of Savoie was able to get this area back, only he had to agree to the condition that the Catholic religion remain forbidden. He accepted, hoping to get his foot in the door. In 1589, the Protestants from Berne invaded again and lost. Only this time, in the peace treaty, the Duke insisted the Catholic Faith be allowed to be taught and followed. The way was opened for Catholics to come in and try to build up the Church again. But the Protestants broke their word and tried to recapture the area without success.

But it was still a stronghold of Calvinism and Calvinists. The situation seemed hopeless. As long as the Calvinists held a grip on the area, neither the Church nor the Duke of Savoie had a chance to bring the people back to the Faith. The Duke asked the bishop to send missionaries at least into the little duchy of Chablais, in an attempt to convert some of those who had turned to Calvinism. In response, the bishop sent a priest, who was from Chablais, thinking he would be acceptable to the people because they knew him. That didn't work, and the priest had to flee for his life.

The bishop called a meeting of his chapter. Without trying

to soft pedal any of it, he explained the problem to them. We don't know why Francis de Sales was the only one who seemed to understand the gravity of the situation. Yet he got up and volunteered to do the job. He spoke very directly and gently, *"My Lord, if you think I'm capable of undertaking this mission, tell me to go. I'm ready to obey and should be happy to be chosen."*[7] He was unanimously accepted, with good reason. No one else wanted the job. However, it was at this point that his father stood up. He appealed to the bishop. His son was only twenty seven years old. He had a bright future ahead of him. Perhaps he wanted to die a martyr's death, but that was not why the Lord brought him into the world. He was so passionate in his plea to the bishop that he was on the verge of calling the whole thing off. (He was not really sold on the project in the first place.) But Francis stood up and convinced the bishop into letting the project go on, as they had planned it.

There were no volunteers other than his cousin Canon Louis de Sales and Francis. On September 14, 1594, the Feast of the Triumph of the Holy Cross, they set forth to win back the Chablais for Jesus. They traveled from Annecy to the border of the Chablais region at which point they sent their horses back. They wanted to be like the apostles, following Jesus' mandate to them, *"Carry no purse, no bag, no sandals; and salute no one on the road...Wherever you enter a town and they receive you, eat what is set before you; heal the sick in it and say to them, `The Kingdom of God has come near to you.'"*[8] They chose to go on foot from that point on.

The remnant of the once great Catholic population, amounted to about twenty scattered individuals, too petrified of the consequences to declare themselves openly. These, Francis worked with and tried to bring back the love of Jesus which they

---

[7]Lives of the Saints - Thomas Plassman OFM - Pg 397
[8]Luke 10:4, 8-9

had known. The raggedy missionaries worked originally in the one town, Thonon, preaching daily, and eventually gradually extending their efforts to the villages in the surrounding countryside. They do remind us of the early travels of Sts. Paul and Barnabas on the island of Cyprus, as written in the Acts of the Apostles. They didn't catch many fish there. The same seemed to apply here.

The cousin, Canon Louis de Sales only lasted four months, after which he went back to Annecy. That left the entire evangelical movement in the province of Chablais to one, Francis. He went through all kinds of struggles, trying to reach the people. He had to walk back and forth from wherever he was to the Château at Allinges every evening because that was where the soldiers and fortifications were maintained. One evening, on his way back, Francis was set upon by wolves, who may have wanted him for dinner. He wound up spending the night in a tree. With the dawn, some peasants found him almost unconscious hanging on for dear life. It was only the Lord who saved him from sure death. Had they not treated him like the Good Samaritan with food and warmed him, he certainly would have died.

As it turned out, they were Calvinists. They were good people; they had just been brainwashed. Francis spoke with such love and compassion to these newly found brothers and sisters, they later converted to Catholicism. Then, of course, he was ambushed by would-be assassins. Apparently, they originally tried to shun him and curse him. When that didn't work, they resorted to physical means. We don't know exactly how the Lord saved him from their attacks, but not only was he saved, but after they were caught, he was able to get their crime pardoned, and they also became converts.

We know that necessity is the mother of invention. Francis had such an urgency to reach many more people than he could physically do, especially since his cousin had left him. So in an effort to find new ways to reach the hearts of the people, he began writing what we would call today, little tracts, explaining the teachings of the Church as opposed to the errors of Calvinism. He spent as much time as he could during the day, writing these little papers, which were then copied many times by hand, and passed out to as many people as possible. *Oh for copy machines!* But he was far ahead of his time. These little tracts, composed under such stress and difficulty, were later to become the basis for his first and most popular book, **Controversies**, one of the reasons he was made a Doctor of the Church. The originals of these pamphlets are still preserved in the archives in the Visitation convent in Annecy.

Something we must point out here is that although Francis de Sales was brilliant, as can be determined by his great education, he wrote and spoke very simply, so that he could be understood by the simplest of minds. Think how important this had to be when he went off evangelizing to the fallen-away Catholics and die-hard Calvinists in the area of Chablais. He had to speak in a way in which they could understand him. In addition, when he wrote these tracts, which became part of Controversies, they were then copied and sent to people who could read them to other groups of Catholics or Calvinists. Not that many people knew how to read in those days. The Printing Press had only begun printing out books towards the middle of this, the Sixteenth Century. So the few who could read would take his tracts, and read them to groups of converts. They had to be simple and theologically sound. Francis was given the gift to be able to do this.

This was the beginning of Francis de Sales, author.[9] After four years, things turned around in the area. Other religious orders sent missionaries into the area. The Catholic Church was on a more solid footing, so the Bishop of Geneva, Claud de

---

[9]He is the Patron Saint of Journalists

Granier, came to visit the mission. He soon saw evidence of the fruits of Francis' self sacrificing work and zeal among the people. The bishop was made welcome and was able to administer Confirmation. He even presided at the Forty Hours Devotion which had seemed unthinkable in Thonen. Through St. Francis' untiring work, the Catholic Faith was reestablished in the province, and he was given the title, *Apostle of the Chablais*.

The Lord touched the heart of the bishop, to consider Francis as his successor. Having had great success against Calvinism in this area of Lake Geneva, it was the right time to bring him before the Pope. When his bishop first suggested this, Francis was not in agreement. His life was too exciting with the work he was doing. He felt he was making great strides; but in the end, he gave in to the wisdom of the bishop, realizing that this was a manifestation of the Lord's Will. He would be able to reach more people, in a position of pastor and authority, as bishop. He also realized it was a dangerous position. He would not be able to go to Geneva. He would have to remain in Annecy until the situation with the Calvinists, who were in complete control, was better. In order for him to receive this great honor, he had to go to Rome to meet with Pope Clement VIII and a full array of bishops and cardinals, including St. Robert Bellarmine. However, the enemy was working fast and furiously. Francis was taken ill. He had to be put to bed for several months. There was a time when it was touch and go. They didn't know for sure if he would survive.

However, the Lord prevailed, and after a period of recuperation, Francis found himself heading for Rome once more, only this time it was in a very official capacity. He was being interviewed by the Pope for the position of Bishop of Geneva. Pope Clement VIII had heard a great deal of the virtue and ability of Francis, not only from the bishop himself, but from various heads of religious orders who had worked with him in the Chablais district of France. The Pope himself, and others, including St. Robert Bellarmine, and a cousin of St. Charles Borromeo, Cardinal Frederick Borromeo, bombarded him with questions on Theology. All of these, he answered with simplicity and modesty, but in a way which proved his learning. What they marveled at was his ability to take the most complex theological questions and answer them in such basic language that the simplest mind could grasp and understand.

He was confirmed as Co-adjutor of Geneva, with the understanding that upon the death of the bishop, he would take that position. Francis returned to take up his work with fresh zeal and energy. However, he couldn't pass Loreto without a visit to his Mother Mary, so in April 1599, Francis returned to Loreto to have some serious conversations with Our Lady. The following morning, he was able to celebrate Mass at the Holy House. He thanked her for all she had done in protecting him from the heretics, and opening up the hearts of the people in the area where he was ministering. He asked her continued support as he began this major step in his life in the church. He prayed the Litany of Loreto, peacefully and serenely. She was by his side.[10]

Pope Clement VIII gave Francis a very exciting proposition. He commissioned him to dialog with Theodore Beza, who was the successor to John Calvin as head of the Calvinists. This would be a great challenge to Francis. But he knew it would take a tremendous amount of Grace to be instrumental in the conversion of the major Calvinist alive at that time. Beza was a brilliant man, who took the edicts of Calvin and enforced them even more strongly than Calvin, if that's possible. He justified everything the Calvinists did. He was able to spread Calvinism far beyond France and Switzerland, but also

---

[10]Our Lady's aid at the Holy House of Loreto was beseeched by many important people in the Church. The year before St. Francis de Sales went there, in 1598, Pope Clement VIII and St. Robert Bellarmine made a pilgrimage there together.

in England, Germany, the Netherlands and central Europe. He made the Calvinist movement more organized, more active in politics, more intellectual and more rigid. Now this was the man whom the Pope believed Francis de Sales could convert back to Catholicism.

Francis was game. He had the strength of Our Lady of Loreto behind him and the confidence of the Pope and many cardinals in Rome as well. He set out to have meetings with Beza. Francis was able to have four meetings with Beza in Geneva. They were lengthy discussions. Francis became very high on Beza's list of respected people. There were times during their meetings that Beza would hesitate, become silent, and ponder greatly on the simplicity but awesome argument the Bishop from Geneva came up with.

Francis felt he would be able to bring Beza over the top with a fifth meeting. But Beza's associates were also able to see the effects Francis was having on their leader. They could not afford to risk losing the head of the movement over a theological victory on the side of the Catholics. They blocked a fifth meeting. Francis persisted, but it never came to pass. Beza died soon after, and his successor had no desire for dialog with the Catholics. It is said that Beza was sad at not having been able to meet with Francis again. But there would have been a lot of changing for him to do to embrace the Catholic Church. He had come too far to turn back. However, we'll never know what that fifth meeting could have accomplished for Francis, Beza, the Church, and Calvinism in France and Switzerland. Oh well, the Lord knows.

In the next few years, he traveled to many places at the request of the bishop to represent the Diocese of Geneva, including Paris in 1602, where he met with the king, Henry IV. The King of Paris was so impressed with Francis that he tried to persuade him to stay in Paris. Francis, however, shared with the king his loyalty to his "poor bride" as he called his little diocese.

The king said of Francis, "the Monseigneur de Genève has every virtue and not a fault."[11]

He had to leave Paris hurriedly as the Bishop of Geneva was dying in the autumn of that year. He was very sad to see the bishop pass on, although he had been showing signs of weakness the past few years. Francis was also a little frightened, although he knew he had the promise of Our Lady of Loreto and her Heavenly Army of Angels, to protect and guide him and his diocese. He committed himself with renewed vigor to the task he had accepted from the Pope three years before. He began in earnest to pastor his people.

We believe that everything we have ever learned is used in the Lord's ministry. We had been salesmen when we were young. We never thought we would use what we had learned as manufacturer's representatives for the Lord. And yet, since we began full-time ministry in 1983, we have used everything we have ever learned. The same applied to Francis de Sales, Bishop of Geneva. He began his career as bishop, using all the Lord had taught him, not only in the four years he worked alone with the people of the Duchy of Chablais, for which he was given the title, Apostle of the Chablais, but what he had learned in school in Paris and Padua. We are somewhat partial, however, when we say we think he learned more in two visits to Our Lady at Loreto than in all the years he spent in school. She prepared him more for what was ahead, and how he was to pastor his flock. So he became very organized in the way he ran his diocese. The more organized he became, the easier things became.

He had a gift of parenting, which is unusual when you consider he was never a parent. We find the same to be true with Mother Angelica who was never a mother, and never had the benefit of a set of parents which she could hold up as role models. And yet she parents her sisters with a great deal of love,

---

[11]Butler's Lives of the Saints Vol I - Pg 199

and they in turn love her. The Bishop of Geneva had the same effect on all those to whom he ministered. Even after his death, people continued to comment on his loving way when he taught Catechism in the parishes in Annecy. However, he was a good parent. When he had to discipline his children, which could include priests, members of nobility, parliament, or whomever, he was a father image. They might not always be happy with his decisions, but they always knew him to be fair.

He had the ability to use the written word extremely well. His tracts which formed his first book, *Controversies*, are proof of this. However, he was able to minister to people on a one-to-one which has brought him a great reputation as a spiritual writer. A series of letters he sent to a relative, Madame de Chamoisy, formed the basis for his most popular book, *Introduction to a Devout Life*. He was able to touch people's hearts through his writings, and they served to put him in places where he could not visit. He reminds us of St. Paul, who had such an urgency to be in an ongoing dialog with his converts. He wrote letters to them, which is how we have some of the most brilliant writing in Scripture, the Letters of St. Paul. Many a convert, among them, St. Augustine, came to the Lord through the writings of St. Paul. The same applies to those who were recipients of the writings of St. Francis. He was persuaded to publish them in a little volume, which, with some additions, first appeared in 1608. The book was at once acclaimed a spiritual masterpiece, and soon translated into many languages.

The Lord put a woman in his path in 1604, Baroness de Chantal, who would become St. Jane Frances de Chantal. She was only thirty two years old at the time and had recently been widowed. He gave her spiritual direction. He could see the Lord working in her life, and when he suggested to her, a few years later, they begin a religious order which would work out in the world, doing corporal works of mercy; she said yes and they began working on it. The name they chose for their order was

Visitation of Our Lady, which came from Our Lady's visit to her cousin Elizabeth, a corporal work of mercy. The charism of the ladies would be to help others in need. Together, they would be responsible for the foundation of the Order of the Visitation in 1610. We will be writing the biography of this Saint in another chapter.

Bishop de Sales became very famous, not only in Annecy and Geneva, but in all of Europe. Being French, he was particularly welcomed by the French nobility. His preaching to members of nobility was responsible for the conversion of many Calvinists and French Huguenots in high places. In 1622, the Duke of Savoy was going to meet Louis XIII in Avignon, and invited Francis to join them there. It was important for Francis to meet with the king, in order to effect some favors for the French part of the diocese. But it was not a good time of the year, Christmastime. Avignon was extremely cold with no way of heating the old Papal Palaces. Also, it seemed he had a premonition that his end was not far off. He actually predicted to his friends that he would never see them again, at which they all became greatly distressed. Before leaving Annecy, he put everything in order, advised his Co-adjutor (who really should have gone in the bishop's place) and went on the trip.

At Avignon, he led as far as possible, his usual austere life. After his meeting with the king, he went to Lyon, a day's distance from Avignon. He stayed at the Convent of the Visitation. But rather than stay in luxurious accommodations, he stayed at a gardener's cottage. Here, for a whole month, though sorely in need of rest, he spared himself no labor. He preached the Christmas day masses. On St. John's Day, he suffered a paralytic seizure and lapsed into a coma. He regained consciousness, and although he recovered his speech, he suffered intensely, which he endured with touching patience. He experienced a great deal of pain with the physicians trying all kinds of remedies to cure him, which only caused more pain and made his end come sooner.

After receiving the Last Sacraments, he laid murmuring words from the Holy Bible, expressing his humble and serene trust in God's mercy. He was heard to say, *"With expectation, I have waited for the Lord, and He heard my prayers, and bought me out of the pit of misery and the filth of mire."*[12]
St. Francis de Sales died at fifty six years old, on December 28, 1622, at eight o'clock in the evening. His body was returned to Annecy where the funeral Mass took place in the Church of the Visitation. His body remains at the gospel side of the altar to this day. His heart, however, was originally placed in a leaden case and enshrined in the Church of the Visitation in Lyon, France. After his beatification, it was changed to a silver case, and now it is in a golden case in the same shrine. The Beatification of St. Francis de Sales in 1662 was the *first* solemn beatification to take place in St. Peter's Basilica in Rome. In 1665, he was canonized; his feast was fixed for January 29th, the anniversary of the bringing of his body to the Visitation in Annecy. He was declared a Doctor of the Church in 1877 and Pope Pius XI named him the Patron Saint of Journalists.

Thus we come to the end of the story of one of the most powerful Saints of the Counter-Reformation. You can see how the life of this Saint is intertwined with the lives of other of the Saints of the Counter-Reformation, either directly or indirectly. Different Saints worked on different fronts, battling the enemy in every way they could. St. Francis de Sales fought the enemies of the Church with the Treasures of the Church,[13] the truths which we have held onto for 2,000 years, and with love. In his wonderful treatise on the love of God, he wrote, *"The measure of*

---

[12]Butler's Lives of the Saints Vol I - Pg 200
[13]To learn about all the *Treasures of our Church,* read Bob & Penny's book of the same name, part of the Trilogy of the Church. Also read *Tragedy of the Reformation,* Book II of the Trilogy, to learn about what happened during the Reformation.

love is to love without measure. "[14]   He certainly practiced what he preached. With that philosophy and the way in which he lived out his philosophy, many conversions came about. Lord, where are our Defenders of the Faith today?

✞✞✞

St. Francis de Sales had a tremendous effect on many famous people throughout Church history. For instance, St. Vincent de Paul, whom St. Francis had entrusted with the first Church of the Visitation in Paris, eulogized him and sent a letter to the Pope, asking for his canonization. He taught from *"Introduction to Devout Life"* at his Thursday night meetings in Paris.

The great devotion to St. Francis de Sales is apparent in St. Don Bosco and his followers. The name of their religious order is the Salesians, in honor of St. Francis de Sales. In addition, there have been other groups, including Missionaries of St. Francis de Sales, the Oblates of St. Francis de Sales, and the Sisters of St. Joseph.

St. John Bosco is the founder of the Salesian Order. We have been asking why he chose St. Francis de Sales as his patron, from the very beginning of our research of Don Bosco. There's no mention in his own writings, or in his biographies, about a significant event in his life, which had anything to do with the Bishop of Geneva; nothing which would give any reason why he chose St. Francis de Sales. Yet there was never a question that his Order would be named after this Saint.

Don Bosco had always been a great *admirer* of St. Francis de Sales. His writings were brilliant. He was a *workaholic*, as was Don Bosco, who fought tirelessly against all the heresies of his day. But possibly the most attractive trait in St. Francis de Sales, which Don Bosco wanted his followers to possess, was his *gentleness and understanding.* The apostolate of Don Bosco

---

[14]Treatise on the Love of God - St. Francis de Sales 1616

was of a very special nature; one where the qualities of gentleness, patience and understanding were as important and possibly more important than any other. He prayed that his benefactor, St. Francis de Sales, would help from Heaven, in instilling these virtues into all his people.

Above: *The wedding of
Saint Jane Frances de Chantal*

Below: *St. Francis de Sales spiritually
directed St. Jane Frances de Chantal.*

Above: *Saint Jane
Frances de Chantal*

Right: *The Order founded by St. Francis
de Sales and St. Jane Frances de Chantal
was involved in caring for the sick.*

St. Jane Frances de Chantal
Co-Foundress of the Visitation Order

Northern Europe was deep into the Protestant Reformation. Luther had done his greatest damage, and had left this earth for his encounter with God the Father and Our Lord Jesus Christ. However, that was not the end of the story. It was really just the beginning. In the wake of Luther came John Calvin who bulldozed the people of Switzerland with his own brand of Protestantism. By 1572, when our future St. Jane Frances de Chantal, nee[1] Frémyot, was born of a noble family in Dijon, Calvinism had taken root firmly not only in Switzerland, but was blazing its way across Holland, and was fighting to create a stronghold in France.

Jane came from a well-to-do family. Her father was the president of the Parliament of the town and district of Burgundy. Sadly, at an early age, her mother died, and her father became the main source of her formation. Since the traumatic loss of her mother, Jane, who added the name Frances for her confirmation name, was tenderly beloved by her father. He tried to make up for the loss of the mother figure in her life. She grew up a very normal girl, versed in all the niceties of the day. She was beautiful, charming, and very gay.

Her father gave her in marriage when she was twenty years old, to Baron Christophe de Rabutin-Chantal, who was then twenty seven years old, an officer in the French Army and an accomplished duelist. The marriage took place in Dijon, after which Jane went with her husband to his home town of Bourbilly, near Semur-en-Auxois, and they settled into his family castle. Since the Baron's mother had died, there had not been a woman's touch in the castle for too many years. Jane provided all the niceties required for a lady in her station. There's nothing in her biography to indicate anything about her spirituality as a young

---

[1]means born; it is often used to indicate maiden name of a married woman

girl. But soon after she took over the castle, the custom of Daily Mass was re-established, which would lead us to believe that she had been used to Daily Mass. After three children had died soon after birth, they were blessed with a boy and three girls.

She was a very level-headed lady, especially considering the fact that she had been spoiled as a child. She never had any desire to impress anyone other than her husband. Because of her beauty, there were always occasions when men would flirt with her, and women would question her about her loyalty to her husband. She made an outstanding statement when one of the other wives commented on the modest clothes the Baroness wore when her husband was away. She simply said, *"The eyes which I want to please are a hundred leagues."*[2] St. Francis de Sales was very impressed with her when they met in 1604. He said of her, *"In Mme. de Chantal, I have found a valiant woman, whom Solomon had difficulty in finding in Jerusalem."*[3]

Her happiness with her husband did not last long, a scarce nine years. One day in 1601, her happy life came to an end when her husband went out shooting. Accidentally he was shot in the thigh. He did not receive good medical treatment, and as a result, he died after nine days of excruciating pain. During that time, Jane had the opportunity to prepare him for death and Heaven. He received all the Sacraments of the Church, and died in the State of Grace. Jane was completely crushed. Her whole life revolved around her husband. They had planned a splendid life together. The nine years they shared were beautiful years.

When she was left a widow at twenty eight years of age, her grief was too intense to be described. For four months, she sunk into deep depression, until she was roused by a letter from her father. He had always been able to reach her. She did the only thing she could under the circumstances; she went home to

---

[2]Butler's Lives of the Saints Vol. III - Pg. 369
[3]Butler's Lives of the Saints Vol. III - Pg. 369

Dijon where she planned to raise her children under the loving eyes of her father. This plan only lasted for a few months before her father-in-law, who was really getting on in age, sent for her to live at his château near Autun. He was a crotchety old man who treated her and the children badly. We don't know for sure why she even went to live with him. She didn't have need. The reason given was that the old man threatened to disinherit her children from their father's estate if she did not live with him. The estate was considerable and she felt she did not have the right to deprive her children of their birthright. So she went and she suffered for over seven years. She and the children suffered silently, like martyrs.

Before Jane had ever met St. Francis de Sales, she had a vision of him. One day she saw a man who looked exactly like St. Francis, same size and features. He was even dressed in the same way St. Francis would dress on the day she actually made his acquaintance. At the time, she was praying to the Lord for a strong Spiritual Director. She had made a private vow not to marry again, but she needed someone to point her in a direction, tell her where to go and what to do with her life.

In 1604, Jane's father advised her that St. Francis was coming to Dijon to give a series of Lenten sermons. She made it a point to leave her father-in-law's home and go to Dijon where she could listen to the Bishop of Geneva, who had an excellent reputation as a speaker. As soon as Jane saw him, she recognized him as the man she had seen in the vision. She had to get him to be her Spiritual Director. Apparently, St. Francis and Jane's father were friendly; because he dined at her father's house often, whenever he was in town; so she had an opportunity to speak to him. She gained a great confidence in him. It was her wish to put her difficulties before him. However, she had made an unwise vow to a Spiritual Director not to discuss her spiritual life with anyone other than this director. However, St. Francis removed her of her responsibility to such an indiscreet vow in short order. She bared her soul to him.

To his way of thinking, she had one overpowering responsibility, which was the raising of her children. They were very young at this time. Also, for their sake, she had to abide by the wishes of her wicked father-in-law at least until the time when the children would be able to be on their own. By his advice, she regulated her devotions and other exercises so as to conform herself to the best interests of her children, and her father and father-in-law. She felt herself being pulled in many directions, but for the sake of the children and in obedience to her new Spiritual Director, she agreed.

She and St. Francis came up with a strict rule of life for her, in which she devoted most of her time to her children, and visited the poor that were sick in the neighborhood and watched whole nights by those who were dying. Sometimes she would return home with the breaking of the dawn after having spent the entire night with a sick or dying person. However, her nocturnal sacrifices and corporal works of mercy could not interfere with her responsibility during the daytime.

St. Francis saw something very special in Jane when he first met her. He knew the Lord had work for her, in conjunction with St. Francis, but he and she would have to wait to find out what the Lord's plan was. It was pretty well determined that she had no intention of remarrying. One day, however, St. Francis was at her father's house. Jane came into the room, dressed extremely well, looking very pretty, as if she were going out on a date, or wanted to impress a suitor. St. Francis looked at her, and commented: *"Madam do you wish to marry again?"* She reeled back, shocked at the suggestion. She answered *"No indeed, my lord!"* at which point he gently said, *"Then you should pull down your flag."*[4] She understood.

Jane Frances had a very difficult time with St. Francis de

---

[4]Butler's Lives of the Saints Vol. III - Pg. 369

Sales as a Spiritual Director. While he was very gentle, he was very firm. He required more from her than from others. She had to die to herself. She was a very strong woman which would work toward God's plan when He was ready to put her into ministry. But the breaking down of who she was, in order to become who she would be, was a great struggle for her. She had always been a firm disciplinarian with her children. She had to soften her relation to and attitude towards them. She had to be more forgiving and less critical. She had a tendency to let loose with a barrage of anger when she had it up to her eyeballs. On St. Francis' instructions, she was not able to vent her temper freely. She had to control her emotions. This would also work in the Lord's favor when He needed it.

For a woman like Jane, she had to make a decision, what she was going to do with her life. She had determined not to marry. But she did not want to live the life of a widow. She was a young, vibrant, alive woman. She wanted to serve the Lord. At times, she considered entering a cloister. That's what women did when they wanted to join religious orders. She asked St. Francis what to do. He had seen an immense need for corporal works of mercy to be performed for people in dire straits, homeless, starving, shut-ins and the like. He took some time to recommend her matter to God, and at the same time, try to discern how he could address the situation of the indigents he saw everywhere. In 1607, the Lord unfolded a plan which would remedy both problems, Jane's desire to do something for the Lord, and St. Francis' project of forming a company, preferably a company of women, who would do the Lord's work under the banner of Mary. He came up with the concept of a congregation of the Visitation of the Virgin Mary. They would follow Mary's example when the Angel Gabriel told her about her cousin Elizabeth. Mary went to Ein Karim to take care of her cousin during her pregnancy. She was completely selfless, not considering her own condition; she concentrated her efforts on being helpful to her cousin, Elizabeth. St. Francis' ladies would take care of people in need.

St. Jane was extremely excited about the project, but still didn't know how she would be able to take care of her father, now aged, who had provided for her needs all her life, and her children, who were still young and her responsibility. To the objection that the obligation which Mme. Chantal owed her children could not be handled, unless she remained with them in the world, St. Francis de Sales replied that they were no longer infants; and in the cloister, she would be able to watch over them with no less vigilance. Perhaps it would be of greater advantage to them, than by continuing to be with them all the time, especially when you consider that the two eldest were about to go into the world. To that end, one daughter married the brother of St. Francis de Sales, and the other two young girls would go with her into the convent. One died shortly after and the other married well within a few years. This still left the father and her son. Her father gave her his blessing, and took on the responsibilities of raising her son, Celse-Bénige, who was fifteen at the time. He would employ the aid of tutors to provide the boy with educational and social skills needed for a young man in his position.

Leaving her father was a difficult proposition for Jane. Remember, they had been best friends all her life, from the time her mother died at an early age. She went out to the porch of her father's home, which she felt she would never see again. She looked at his aged face. She was sure, also, that this was the last time they would speak to each other in this life. His eyes were filled with tears, as were hers. He laid his hands on her head and gave her his blessing. Then he took her face in his hands. *"I cannot blame you for what you do. You go with my consent, and I offer you to God, a daughter dear to me as ever Isaac was to Abraham. Go where God calls you. I shall be happy, knowing you are in His house. Pray for me. "*[5]

St. Francis set up a house, called the Gallery House, on the edge of Lake Annecy, for Jane and two other girls, who would make up the core of his new community. He inaugurated his convent on Trinity Sunday in 1610. Jane Frances was clothed with two other sisters that day. Pretty soon more came and in short order there were twelve visiting nurses. But there was a problem from the outset. The people would not accept nuns in habits walking the streets. Nuns were in cloistered convents. They did not take part in social work, even if it was, as the beloved Bishop of Geneva called it, "Corporal Works of Mercy." If they were to be nuns, they had to be in cloister.

St. Francis changed the plan of the congregation to conform to the need of making it an enclosed religious order under the rule of St. Augustine. Actually, he wrote the rule and constitution for the community, which is not unusual. He was the bishop of the diocese in which they would be housed. He made the cornerstone of the community of sisters, Humility and Meekness. He told them, *"In the practice of virtues, let humility be the source of all the rest; let it be without bounds; make it the reigning principle of all your actions. Let an unalterable meekness and sweetness on all occasions become by habit natural to you."*[6] But he refused to give up the name of the Visitation of Our Lady, which he had chosen for his sisters, and St. Jane Frances urged him to make no concessions at all.

A powerful teaching he gave to St. Jane and her ladies had to do with how they treated Calvinists and other heretics. He said, *"I have always said that whoever preaches with love is preaching effectively against the heretics, even though he does not say a single controversial word against them."*[7]

Jane founded eighty seven monasteries between 1615 and

---

[5]Butler's Lives of the Saints Vol. III - Pg. 371
[6]Teaching to St. Jane and her Visitation Nuns by St. Francis de Sales
[7]Butler's Lives of the Saints - Volume I - Page 198

1641. She traveled on horseback or a litter to found or visit new communities. She was very close to ordinary people, and the residents of Annecy venerated her. Ann of Austria asked her to bless her son, who became the future Louis XIV. In 1641, she went into France on an errand of charity. She was invited by the queen to Paris, and to her distress, was treated there with great distinction and honor.

Returning home, she fell on the way to her convent in Moulins, and was taken there to recuperate. However, she died there on December 13, 1641 at sixty-nine years of age. Her body was taken down to Annecy, and buried near St. Francis de Sales. She was canonized in 1767. St. Vincent de Paul said of her,

"She was full of faith, and yet all her life, had been tormented by thoughts against the faith. While apparently enjoying that peace and easiness of minds of souls who have reached a high state of virtue, she suffered such interior trials and she often told me her mind was filled with all sorts of temptations and abominations that she has to strive not to look within herself for she could not bear it.

"The sight of her own soul horrified her as if it were an image of hell. But for all that suffering, her face never lost its serenity, nor did she want to relax the fidelity God asked of her. And so I regard her as one of the holiest souls I have ever met on this earth."[8]

And this from one Super Saint, about another Super Saint!

---

[8]Butler's Lives of the Saints - Volume III - Page 373

St. Vincent de Paul

Apostle of the Poor and Homeless

Our cry rings out to the whole world. Take notice! *We are in the times of great Saints in the making. We are in the times of unequaled sinners.* Enemies of God, we put you on notice: We've been there before; we've suffered the arrows of persecution in times past and we are still here. We are not finished. For the last 2000 years, just as it appeared the end was near, the Church was about to collapse, the world was coming to an end, God raised up *Super Saints,* those who said Yes to God's call to holiness. One such great Saint in the making, one soul who reached for and received the crown of glory in Heaven, was St. Vincent de Paul.

In the history of the Church, we find The Lord *very often raising the lowly to confound the proud.*[1] The Church is in need! All of Europe is being devastated by the onslaught of Calvinism and Lutheranism. The Heresy of Albigensianism[2] that had its beginning in Albi, the south of France, had left its scars of division, even hundreds of years after it was condemned. Now, there was the threat coming from their neighbors to the north - Germany, Switzerland and the Nordic countries. People were confused; often their priests did not live what they preached and so the faithful stopped going to church. Would He lose these precious souls? God raised up another Saint and, through his living out of the Gospel, a Defender of the Faith. France, eldest daughter of the Church, would give the world and the Church a Seventeenth Century Mother Teresa.

---

[1] cfLk 1:52

[2] More on this heresy and other heresies the Church fought and won, throughout her 2000 year history, read Bob and Penny Lord's book: *Scandal of the Cross and It Triumph, Heresies throughout the history of the Church.*

Above: *St. Vincent De Paul*

Above: *St. Vincent De Paul Apostle of the Poor*

Left: *St. Vincent De Paul in Glory*

Below: *The Incorrupt body St. Vincent De Paul in Paris, France*

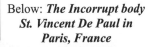

A farmer's son sows seeds which will grow into a beautiful spiritual bouquet in the garden of the Lord.

In southern France, close to the Spanish border, in the small village of Pouy, the family of a future Saint was expecting the birth of their third child. This day, a little bitter from the cold and dampness, would be brightened by the cry of a baby boy, as he takes his first peek at the world outside the safety of his loving mother's womb. The Saint, we want to tell you about, our dear St. Vincent de Paul, was that baby! Born under humble circumstances, into a family of poor farmers, St. Vincent would always have a special place in his heart and his vocation for the poor, whether physically or spiritually deprived.

God placed this special child in the hands of holy parents, poor in the foolish eyes of the world, but rich in their faith. Vincent's parents did not wait to have their baby baptized! Instead, a few short days after he was born, they brought him to their local parish to be initiated into the Church, receiving the first of the seven Sacraments, the *Sacrament of Baptism*. These parents of a future Saint were eager to have their newborn son begin his life not only as their son, but more importantly as a son of God; and to insure this, their focus was to have the priest quickly wipe him clean of the stain of Original Sin, that he would be ready to begin his journey on earth leading to Paradise and eternal life with a Heavenly Family.

The seed of faith, which had been planted by God would now be nurtured by this holy family. Holiness was evident in Vincent from infancy; his family said that from his earliest years, he would become elated when he was praying. As a child, he could be heard singing and praying the psalms, as he tended the cattle in the fields.

Jean de Paul, little Vincent's father, had to work hard; the land was dry and parched when there was too little sun and did not yield a good crop; and when there was too much rain and not enough sun the crops were flooded and the results were always the same; too much work for too little return. Often the land did not yield enough to feed the livestock, no less the family. Out of necessity, the boy Vincent, along with his five brothers and sisters helped out the family, by working on the farm.

Vincent was assigned to watch over the sheep. As a young shepherd he early devised a way to tend his charges, even during the rainy season. When the land became so soaked, he could not walk without sinking up to his knees in the mud, Vincent improvised! He took some sticks of wood and made them into stilts; they raised him about three feet from the ground. His life story does not go into how many times he fell and got up again; all we do know is that he learned to balance himself and joyfully went about his appointed responsibilities. Through his new-found elevation, he not only remained dry, he was able to care for his flock, surveying the fields, guarding and counting each head, lest one should wander off and get lost. We can see God preparing Vincent for the walk he would have as pastor of a human flock.

Young Vincent and his love for the poor

What is one man's suffering is another man's joy; for as God, the Author of life, can turn dead seeds into sweet smelling blooms, God can turn what would appear a distasteful situation into an asset. There are times when out of necessity, if compromise is inevitable, farmers will build the barn better than the house. With the de Paul family, the barn was *attached* to the house, with only a split door separating the members of the *barnyard* family from the *human* family. It turned out to be a blessing in disguise, the body heat of the cows and other livestock furnishing much needed warmth in the winter; and when it was too inclement for man or beast in the yard, the family was able to feed their four-legged friends through the upper opening in the split door.

The de Paul family took care to not only labor earnestly to provide for the needs of the flesh, but at day's end, to provide food for the soul. After the meal was over, all gathered around the fireplace in the kitchen (where they also slept); the father told them stories of the lives of the Saints; they all prayed together, offering praise and thanksgiving for their daily bread and supplicating the Lord to continue granting them what they need. As their parents tucked them into bed, the children would ask them for their blessing. [Do we bless our families before they go to sleep? Is our blessing the last thing our families bring with them when they leave the house?]

Although poor, Vincent's parents were generous. Each Sunday, during the Sacrifice of the Mass when the time came for the Offertory, they placed what little money they had in the basket. In addition, no matter how hard the times, they always found money to give to those less fortunate than they. Vincent grew up with this holy example, always remembering Jesus' words, *"Whatever you do to the least of My brothers, that you do unto Me."*[3]

From the time he was a young boy, Vincent saw Jesus in the faces of the poor. This would mold his noble heart into the life he would be called to, as advocate of the poor. One time, Vincent had saved thirty pieces of silver. He had dreamed about what he would buy for his family to make life a little easier. Then one day, Vincent encountered a poor beggar on the road; without a moment's hesitation Vincent gave the poor soul all the silver he had. Had he seen Jesus? Was this his way of placing no one before the Lord. *Whoever gives up mother and father...*[4]

At an early age, his mother instructed Vincent to turn to his *Heavenly* Mother, sharing all his joys and sorrows, his wounds and his triumphs, confident She would never let him down. As was the custom of other children of the area, Vincent built a little shrine to Mother Mary in a tree. There he would pour out his heart to her. He and his family would go on pilgrimage once or twice a year to a shrine to Notre Dame,[5] in

---

[3]*cf*Mt 25:40
[4]*cf*Mt 19:29
[5]Our Lady

Buglose. On the way they would encounter other Frenchmen going to venerate their Mother; some petitioning and others responding with thanksgiving for prayers answered. Vincent remarked, later in life, that he could not remember Our Lady not answering his prayers. He taught that the more we love the Blessed Mother, the more we love Jesus, the happier we will be.

Vincent begins his journey to the priesthood

Vincent showed a thirst and aptitude for learning, which was further enhanced by a truly virtuous soul. When he was interviewed by the Bishop, to see if he qualified to receive First Holy Communion, he answered so brilliantly and authentically, the Bishop not only said he was ready, but encouraged the parents to send him to the city to further his education. His father responded by scraping together what little he had, to secure an education for this special son, with the Cordeliers or Franciscan Recollects.

Life at the college for Vincent was like a dream come true; he absorbed Grammar and Latin like a sponge; he excitedly looked forward to each day, like a child awaiting Christmas. What with his remarkable ability to learn and his humble and always eager desire to help, his joyful *Yes* to all in need, he became a friend and example to the other students at the College.

As you cannot hide a light under a bushel basket; he came to the attention of Mr. Commet, a nobleman of the village who asked him to tutor his children This overjoyed Vincent as what little he earned would enable him to cease being a financial burden on his parents. After four years he shared with Mr. Commet that he found himself drawn to the priesthood. Monsieur encouraged him to go answer the Lord's call to serve Him as an *"alter Christus."*[6] Mr. Commet advised Vincent's father of his son's desire to become a priest, and he immediately sold two of his steers.

In 1596, at sixteen years of age, Vincent entered the

---

[6]another Christ in Latin

University of Toulouse, where he studied and prepared for the priesthood. Shortly after entering, he received the tonsure.[7] He was among the young men who that day were vested in the Franciscan habit and received into the Order of St. Francis. The Bishop cut his hair along with that of the other future priests present, and Vincent was no longer a lay man; he had taken his first step; he was now a cleric! After receiving minor orders, the Subdiaconate and then the Diaconate, on September 23, 1600, at less than twenty years old,[8] Vincent realized his dream; he was ordained a Priest; he was no longer Vincent, but Father Vincent. He returned to the little chapel at the beginning of the woods, where he prayed as a little boy, and fervently celebrated his first Mass there.

St. Vincent's walk was the living out of the Gospel. Like St. Francis, his focus in life was to be more like Jesus. But initially he sought Jesus, studying the Word of God and the Traditions of the Church. The more he did, the more he *became* the Gospel. Although he desired to continue his studies, the lack of funds and the debt he had incurred, when he was preparing for the priesthood, did not permit him to do so. But his holiness and generosity toward the poor came to the attention of a good woman who bequeathed her estate to him. Upon her death, he would receive 500 crowns of silver!

Now, the only problem was that this sum was owed to the departed by an unscrupulous debtor. He had fled to Marseille in order to avoid paying the woman. Vincent knew that the only way he could hope to collect his inheritance was to seek out the debtor and appeal to him to pay. In 1605, Vincent left for Marseille to retrieve his inheritance!

---

[7]In this ceremony the Bishop cuts snips of hair from the front, back, two sides and the crown, as an invitation by the candidate to accept the Lord as his only portion. In some orders the top of the head leaving a crown of hair solely on the top of the head. This is a permanent sign of his commitment.
[8]Today, a priest is not ordained until close to twenty seven years old, but in the days of Vincent de Paul the age was more like twenty four.

In Marseille, he found the scoundrel, only to have him offer far less than the debt he owed; but having wisdom, St. Vincent accepted the paltry sum and prepared to return to Toulouse. A young gentleman staying in the same inn as Vincent, suggested he book passage on the boat he was taking to Narbonne. As this fit his budget and would save him time, Vincent joyfully accepted.

Vincent is sold into slavery

The two new-found friends boarded the ship; the voyage began smoothly; the sun was shining; the Mediterranean Sea was calm; all was well aboard the ship. But suddenly, ominously in the horizon loomed three ships carrying the colors of the Saracens. They signaled the ship, advising the French to prepare for them to board her. No sooner had they finished coming aboard, the Saracen pirates began fighting immediately. Although the French sailors, along with Vincent who joined in, fought bravely, they were greatly out-numbered and the ship was soon taken over. Vincent's dream of returning home was now a horrible nightmare; the deck, brilliantly lit earlier by the rays of the sun, was now covered with blood and lifeless bodies. The wounded Vincent and those not killed were taken prisoners and placed in chains for the rest of the voyage.

At the end of eight days, after the pirates had satisfactorily benefited from other piracies, they arrived in Tunisia. Now, Vincent was penniless, the Saracens having stripped him and all aboard of all their possessions. When they landed, in order to not be challenged by the French authorities, the pirates falsely claimed they had taken the slaves (Vincent was one of them) from a Spanish ship. They paraded them around the port, offering them for sale. Having no takers, they brought them to the livestock auction where animals were bought and sold. The prospective buyers probed and inspected the Christians, just as they would animals. They opened their mouths, inspected their teeth; they looked them over, as they would a steer or goat. When the auctioneer asked for bids, the buyers offered less than for a beast of burden.   Finally, Vincent was bought by a fisherman.   As Vincent was not a good sea traveller, he soon became sick and useless to the fisherman, and was returned to the market, to once again suffer the humiliation of being auctioned off like a side of beef. Vincent was sold to an elderly physician.   Now the physician was kind and quickly learned to love Vincent, like a son.   He paid him a fair wage and did not treat him as a slave.   There were some problems; the good doctor was deeply interested in magic and wanted to ingrain this sorcery in Vincent; in addition, he tried to share all the knowledge he had amassed, his fifty years of research in alchemy;[9] and if that was not bad enough, being a Moslem, he tried endlessly to convert Vincent to Islam!   Vincent prayed to Our Lady, tirelessly begging to be delivered from the temptations that were assailing him; it would be so easy to give in; he was so tired of fighting.   But he had his Mother Mary! Later speaking of this time, he gave full credit for his victory over the seductions that lambasted him to Mary.

The doctor was invited by the Grand Sultan to visit him in Constantinople.   In spite of his age, this was an invitation, the good doctor could not refuse.   The old man died enroute and Vincent was now the chattel of the doctor's nephew who had inherited him as part of the legacy.   It was August, 1606, and Vincent had lost the only kind person he had met, since being taken prisoner.   The nephew was as cruel and heartless, as his uncle had been kind and generous.   But God is always listening and never gives us more than we can bear.   The nephew wanted no part of his uncle's businesses and sold all he had inherited, including Vincent.

The nephew heard that the French ambassador to Turkey was arriving with an authorization to free all the French citizens who had been sold into slavery, so he quickly sold Vincent to Niçois, a former Christian who had become an apostate to escape

---

[9]the science of changing metal into gold

the fate of Christian captives. To avoid being sold into slavery or sentenced to death, Niçois had renounced his religion and became a follower of Mohammed. Now, the Sultan was generous to the apostate; he rewarded him for his apostasy by presenting him with property and a grand vacation home in the mountains. But none of this made Niçois happy. He wandered aimlessly, seeking some peace in his soul.

Niçois brought Vincent to the desert where he worked under the broiling heat, radiated by the sun on the white sand. Although he was not mistreated, his food and lodging were very poor. But Vincent offered up all his suffering for the conversion of the apostate. As he worked, Vincent unceasingly sang to the Blessed Mother, invoking her aid.

Niçois had three wives, one of whom was Moslem. In her own right, she was very spiritual, praying to Allah five times a day. As she watched Vincent laboring under the hot sun, her heart was moved to pity. She silently grieved over his captivity and the conditions he lived under. She could see he was a good and holy man, and was impressed by his peace, the peace her husband did not have. She could not help marveling at Vincent's strength, his acceptance of his state in life.

She found herself drawn to Vincent's holy demeanor, as she listened to his chanting of the Psalms, the Salve Regina, and the Divine Office, as he went about doing his work. She asked Vincent to translate the chants, especially the Salve Regina. Vincent, with all the ardor he had stored up, began to teach her about Jesus and the Catholic Faith. The woman would look into Vincent's tear-filled eyes, as he spoke of his Lord Who came to the earth to save all men, and she could feel all the love he had for his God. One night, she excitedly recounted to her husband, all that Vincent had told her. Then she began scolding her husband for having left his religion, saying she could not understand how he could deny such a loving God and abandon a beautiful religion which teaches love and compassion. She was to be the instrument which God would use to release her husband from the bondage of apostasy.

The following morning, the apostate sought out Vincent; he fell down on his knees, confessed all that he had done and told Vincent he wanted to return to his Faith. Vincent said the only way he would achieve peace was to return to France where Niçois could do penance for his sins. Months later the two, under the cover of night, clandestinely escaped to France, landed in Marseille and finally arrived in Avignon. It just happened to be that the vice-legate of the Pope lived in Avignon. There, in the church of St. Peter, the fallen Christian made peace with the Church. Niçois shared his desire to make penance for his grave sins. The legate, impressed by his sincerity helped him to enter the Monastery of the Brothers of Charity, where he remained serving the sick in the hospital, until his death. Vincent left for Rome.

Vincent having gained the patronage of the vice-legate, who gave him letters of introduction, remained in Rome for quite a time. The Vatican was awesome for Vincent; here was the holy land upon which the center of his Faith rested, his Church nourished by the blood of Martyrs. His eyes welled up with tears, and his voice choked with emotion, as he filed past the tombs of Popes, who had served the Church in unbroken succession, beginning with the first Pope - St. Peter.

St. Vincent returns to Paris and knows persecution.

He could have stayed and basked in the glory that was Rome, but knew he had to go on to Paris. News of Vincent de Paul's involvement in the conversion of the apostate came to the attention of Pope Paul V[10] and in 1608, Vincent was commissioned to go to Henry IV on a confidential mission. Vincent departed for Paris, poste-haste.

Because Vincent was not otherwise employed, the King asked him to be the Queen's chaplain. The Queen told the King she sincerely repented her past conduct and wanted to change her

---

[10]via his vice-legate from Avignon

life, and that she gladly accepted Father Vincent as her Spiritual Director and confessor. The Queen became very devoted; soon everyone looked upon her with admiration. Her selfishness replaced by selflessness, her life became filled with great acts of mercy and charity.

Queen Margot entrusted Father Vincent with the task of distributing great sums of silver to the poor and visiting the sick in the Hospital of Charity. Now, although Father preferred visiting the poor, he obeyed the Queen and ministered to the nobility. It was on such an occasion, he met King Henry IV's son, the Dauphin and future King Louis XIII. While in the service of Queen Margot, Father Vincent returned to his interrupted studies and followed the lessons being given at the Sorbonne, with the idea of receiving a degree in Canon Law. He studied industriously, but never at the expense of his duty to the Queen and the poor. He distributed large sums to the poor, never keeping a coin for himself. He refused to live in the Palace.

Vincent chose to board, out of humility, in a modest lodging in the area of St. Germain. It was owned by a Judge of the Tribunal, Monsieur de Sore. Vincent was so happy, but his peace was to be short-lived. One day, when Vincent was sick in bed, with a fever (from an illness contracted in Africa), the Judge entered the room and, as was his custom, placed a large sum of money in the safe. But in a hurry and somewhat distracted, instead of leaving the key in a safe place, he left it on the server. Later the delivery boy from the pharmacy brought medicine to Father Vincent. Upon seeing him sound asleep, and noticing the key, he opened the safe and stole all the contents. On his return, the judge seeing the safe ajar and his money gone, accused Vincent.

Although Vincent calmly protested he was innocent, he was not able to prove it; he was not believed and was to bear the stigma of being a thief for *six years*. During the six long years, without friends, and anyone who believed in him, he never endeavored to defend himself. He just bore the scandal, resignedly repeating over and over again, *"God knows the truth."* Finally six years after the fact, the truth always surfacing, the criminal was arrested for another crime and, wanting to clear his conscience, confessed to the crime Vincent had been accused of. St. Vincent never told anyone of his ordeal. Instead he used this as a teaching on retreats. Without using any names, he stressed the positive rather than remember and dwell on the negative, teaching that we can sustain the pain of false accusations, which pierce our hearts, by remembering always that God in His timetable will reveal the truth, if it is His Will. Thank God, even if it was after six years, that in Vincent's case, it was God's Will!

Vincent meets a holy priest and his life takes a new course

Not all was sad in Paris, for St. Vincent. There he met up with a holy priest, Father de Bérulle, who would later become a Cardinal. Again we see God the Omnipotent Chessman putting His chess pieces in position, lining them up to serve Him and His Church. Father De Bérulle asked St. Vincent to serve as Curé of a small parish outside Paris. Then he commissioned him to be Spiritual Director to Countess Joiguy and serve as teacher to her children.

St. Vincent was a champion of the Sacraments, preaching often on most especially the Sacrament of Penance. One day, when the countess was away on a trip, someone came to St. Vincent and asked him to hear the confession of a man who was dying. Before administering Extreme Unction (or the Sacrament of the Sick as it is now called), St. Vincent asked the man to make a general confession. When he helped the man examine his conscience, St. Vincent discovered the man had previously made imperfect confessions. Because he had not properly examined his conscience, this rendered his former confessions sacrilegious.

When Countess Joiguy returned and her subject told her that he might have died with sins on his soul, had St. Vincent not prepared him, she begged St. Vincent to preach that Sunday in their country church on the Feast of the Conversion of St. Paul. After his homily, the people flocked in such great numbers to have their confessions heard, St. Vincent had to ask the local Jesuits for help.[11]

The time came when Father de Bérulle told Vincent it was time to leave the countess' home and serve the common people who were in such dire need of spiritual nourishment. Gathering five other priests, Vincent formed a little community and they began converting many back to the true Faith, calling them (including royalty) to cease living scandalous lives painful to God. Countess Joiguy was in full accord with the great work that Vincent was doing; but she made him promise he would always be available, he would never abandon the care of her soul, and he would be there to help her at the moment of her death. Always devoted to those whom God entrusted to her, the countess convinced her husband to support Vincent's Company of missionaries who would help their peasants and teach them how to live a better life.

Violence deals a blow to France which leaves her lamenting!

May 14, 1610, was a sad day in the history of France, for on this day, King Henry IV was assassinated. The whole world was shocked and grief-stricken. Cardinal de Bérulle asked Father Vincent and another holy priest to come and study with him, how to restore France to her heritage as a holy Christian country. For fifteen years France had been suffering terribly from the devastating religious wars which had attacked and were now crippling her. Upon carefully studying the problem, the Cardinal, decided to found a *Society of the Oratory* in *France*, fashioned after that of Philip Neri in *Italy*.

Vincent spent a year at the *Oratory*, when he was asked by the Curé of the church in Clichy to take over as pastor. On May 2, 1612, Vincent became Curé of this parish outside Paris. The parish was badly neglected, with few attending Mass.

---

[11]St. Vincent's Congregation has celebrated January the 15th as a solemn Feast Day from that day till today, in commemoration of this momentous occurrence in their community's history.

Vincent recalled the original peasants with whom he had felt so at home, the simple believers who loved their church. Now the church was in great need of repair, the parishioners as well as the church building which was falling down. His first sermon was on his plans to restore the church and as the parish grows to build a larger one to accommodate the additional believers. St. Vincent began to teach catechetics; the congregation joined him singing beautiful chants during the Mass, and before you knew it the church was too small!

One day, on his way to pay a visit to a family living in a château, Vincent met the lady who would before too long, become co-founder of his Daughters of Charity, Louise de Marillac.[12] Wherever he went, he was well-loved by the people; he was bringing to them, the Jesus for Whom they had been starving, without knowing it. But that too was to come to an end, when in less than a year, he was asked by Cardinal de Bérulle to move on. His parishioners accompanied him out of town, weeping at their loss; and he for his part, said he would never forget them and his time with them. He never did!

St. Vincent is again taken away from his beloved poor

Cardinal de Bérulle advised Vincent that his new mission was of paramount importance, as it concerned Monsieur de Gondi, the Commander in Chief of the Navy and Prince of the realm. When he asked the Cardinal for an outstanding tutor for his children, he had recommended Father Vincent. Now, although he had left his heart with the peasants in Clichy and his life to serve the poor and disadvantaged, he obeyed! Although he did not initially understand this latest Will of the Lord, he would in time see His plan; Father Vincent, through his relationship with the royal family would meet the wealthy and influential who would become patrons of what he would begin later.

In the beginning his time was spent mainly with the children, but soon he was speaking to the servants about Jesus

---

[12]Her tomb is in the Chapel of the Miraculous Medal in Paris.

their Savior. Then it was time for the master of the château! Watching his dedication, his goodness, the influence he had on his children and others of his household, the Count's respect for Vincent grew so much that he began to count on him for guidance.

Before going to engage in a duel, one day, the Count asked Father Vincent if he could attend his Mass. When the Mass was over, Father Vincent went down on his knees and told the Count that he knew he was going to engage in a duel. Vincent demanded, in the Name of the Lord, he desist from this act of violence; and should he not obey, the good Lord would bring down His justice upon the Count and his posterity. What Vincent was proposing was contrary to the lifestyle required of a noble, as part of the royal family and the King's Court. Monsieur de Gondi had never heard anyone speak to him in this fashion, with such strength and courage. Right there, he pledged to God to never duel again. The Count spoke of this incident and soon the entire court was talking about the Curé. They followed the Count's example and became benefactors of St. Vincent's apostolate.

Soon, his wife asked Father Vincent for Spiritual Direction. Although she was well known for her piety, her spirit was disquieted. After she confessed to Father Vincent, she had peace. She asked him to guard her soul, from that time on, by giving her direction. Now, Madame de Gondi had peasants in Picardie and unhappily they were much neglected. With no priests, there was no Mass, no Sacraments, no guidance; God was no longer *Someone*, He became *something* of the past. Madame asked Father Vincent to preach to her people. He did with such force and fire, soon there were long lines waiting to go to confession.

Vincent goes to the physically and spiritually impoverished.

All in order, Father Vincent knew it was time to follow his heart and organize missions to the poor. He felt an excitement and it was with much urgency that he asked Cardinal de Bérulle for his blessing. He came just as the Cardinal received a communication begging for help in an important parish in the region of Châtillon-les-Dombes. Vincent was sent! He said au revoir to his tearful charges and assured them he would pray for them, and that they needed no one but the Good Lord Who is watching over them. It was with mixed feelings he was on his way; he had grown to love this little family and would miss them; but his heart was beating wildly in anticipation of his new assignment; he was on his way to serve the poor, at last!

What this Curé found was a foretaste of what St. John Vianney walked into in Ars, in a later century. There was no one to greet him; the people had become impious, indifferent to the Church and finally to God. The parish church was in horrible disrepair; no more was it used by man to worship his Lord; instead the four-legged animals were making God's home, their home. The Curé of Ars, said, *"Take away the priest and the people will worship animals."* Father Vincent found the Catholics in the village were few; whereas the Protestants were many. The few Catholics he met were unfriendly, without compassion, weak and self-seeking. The village, like many in Europe, was fractured by the division that had come about through the influx of Calvinism into a once Catholic community. The new Curé would have his hands full!

As the rectory was occupied by the poor and homeless who had no other home to go to, Father went over to the hotel, looking for a place to stay. Jean Beynier, the owner was friendly and Protestant! Respecting his wishes, the new Curé guarded what he said. But the owner, seeing over the weeks the abundance of the Curé's kindness to all, and his deep sincerity, was won over by him, converted to the Faith and became one of the Curé's staunchest supporters. Father Vincent did not look upon the Protestants as enemies but as brothers.

Father did the same as he had done in Clichy; he taught them catechism with so much ardor and passion the Catholics were proud to be Catholic; the Protestants began coming to the

little church, converted and the numbers grew and grew! No
more baying and mooing of four-legged creatures inside the
sanctuary; those whom God had created in *His* Image now sang.
The church sounded as if it was filled with the voices of Angels
mingling with those of humans. People, as in Clichy, came from
far and near to attend the Mass and participate in all the activities
of this church which was alive!

One Sunday morning, just as Father was about to celebrate
the Sacrifice of the Mass, someone ran in and told him that there
was a family who was very ill, with no one to care for them.
With no one to cook for them, the children were starving! Father
Vincent spoke so passionately of the plight of the family, that
very afternoon what should he see, from these former apathetic
villagers, but families going back and forth bringing help and
provisions to the family in need. Father Vincent commended
them, but said now they had to devise a system where they would
continue to care for the family until they were able to care for
themselves. And the people responded, Parishioners and
Protestants, alike. The house of God was no longer divided;
almost all in the village, in less than five months became
Catholic.

When he instructed the people how to serve the poor, he
said it is not *what* you give but *how* you give it. When you give,
see Jesus before you and then serve His children how you would
serve Him. At last, Vincent was doing what he was born to do!
Then he received word from his good friends, the de Gondi
family, that they needed him. As he had heard no word from the
Bishop of Paris, before responding, the Curé asked Cardinal de
Bérulle for permission. That granted, once again Vincent
obeyed! Those who had been touched by him were saddened by
his departure, but they were changed; he had touched their lives,
given them a new way to live, and they would not forget!

St. Francis de Sales enters St. Vincent de Paul's life.

It's 1618, and as the Lord would have it, St. Vincent de
Paul made the acquaintance of St. Francis de Sales. Now, St.

Francis de Sales, had become known as *the holy Bishop of Geneva.* He and the faithful of Switzerland had suffered greatly when his diocese became the cradle of Calvinism.[13] Years before the enemy struck, first *ideologically* and that failing - *physically* - St. Francis de Sales had founded the Order of the Visitation whose charism was to visit the poor and the sick. He had shared this dream with St. Jane Frances de Chantal. But as it was not permitted, at that time, for sisters to come and go from their convents, there was nothing St. Francis could do, but forsake his project. The sad truth is, should the Church have granted the sisters leave to visit the poor and infirmed, it would not have been prudent in any case, what with the violence being visited upon those who resisted the zealot Calvinists, in Geneva.

The sisters being cloistered, could not leave the convent. What were the options? Open a boarding schools for girls! But who was to teach them? The holy bishop and St. Jane Frances de Chantal asked St. Vincent de Paul to be the Spiritual Director of the Visitation of Paris, the school where the daughters of the nobility would board and receive an education. Although eager to be with the poor, St. Vincent agreed, out of obedience to the bishop and respect of their friendship. For the most part, the students, touched by his strong witness grew more fervent, in some cases, than his strongest collaborators. The young socialites went out on missions of mercy and God's plan began to take form. St. Francis de Sales died the 29th of December, and St. Vincent de Paul became St. Jane Frances' Spiritual Director. But his commitments to the Visitation Sisters and their foundress, did not deter St. Vincent from serving the sick and the poor.

St. Vincent de Paul never stopped taking seriously his mission to distribute resources to the poor, and offer hope and shelter to the homeless and forgotten. When men became rare, who would work at shoveling coal into the furnaces of ships, the

[13]read more on Calvin and Calvinism in Bob and Penny Lord's book: *Tragedy of the Reformation*

French navy took prisoners and, under the most inhumane conditions, subjected them to forced labor aboard the ships. Hearing of their plight, St. Vincent visited them. He went into the holds of the ships where they suffocated from the heat and lack of air; into the prisons, cold and dank, where they hopelessly awaited their fate, as slaves on board the ships, working in the holds shoveling coal into hungry furnaces.

St. Vincent de Paul not only ministered to them, the abandoned; but upon seeing the deplorable conditions, the rats and vermin in the jails, the lack of sanitation, St. Vincent fought, crying out *vehemently* against man's total inhumanity toward his fellow man. He reached the ears of his powerful benefactors; who thereupon visited the jails, and conditions were improved! The prisoners, seeing the kindness and real caring of St. Vincent went to confession and began their walk back to God and His Church; St. Vincent had shown them there is a God of love and they had hope!

An old friend goes Home

In 1625, his loyal friends Count and Countess de Gondi made a will leaving the budding Society of St. Vincent de Paul a considerable inheritance: 45,000 books.[14] In addition to this, at their bidding, the Count's brother, Archbishop John Francis Gondi of Paris, gave the new community a college to house their new institution, with the Count and Countess generously providing the necessary funds. The Archbishop had only one condition, he required that the new Congregation commit to providing relief to the needy out in the countryside, as well as in Paris, and spiritual assistance to convicts, all at no charge. In April, 1625, St. Vincent and his company took possession and St. Vincent was on his way.

A good friend goes Home! On the 23rd of June, 1625, two months after the founding of the Mission, the Countess de Gondi went to her Lord, at forty two years of age. She had tried to do

---

[14]a large inheritance for that time, as books were so rare

God's Will as she understood His Will, and now the Lord, in response to her generous heart took His daughter by the hand and led her peacefully Home. She had her wish; she died, comforted by the presence of her beloved Spiritual Director Father Vincent de Paul. True to his promise, he had attended the countess right to the last moments of her life; having done so, he was free to join his congregation.

Her husband was not with her when the Countess closed her eyes for the last time. It fell to Father Vincent to bring him the sad news. Now, the Count, like his wife, had become very spiritual; he resignedly accepted his wife's death as God's Will. But this premature death of his dear wife showed him how meaningless the treasures of this world were and he asked to be admitted into the newly founded Congregation of Priests of the Mission. As Father Vincent de Paul had not the authority to grant this, he suggested instead that the Count become a disciple of Cardinal de Bérulle and priest of the Oratory.

The work greater than the workers, God sends help!

Many houses opened, all over France, in Montpellier, Périqueux, Montauban, Troyes, Annecy, Marseille and too many to list here. God blessed this selfless work. Members of the Royal Court took up where the Countess de Gondi had left off; so many of the houses of our Daughters of Charity were run by these ladies. They visited the sick and the abandoned, offering solace and compassion. They went into hospitals totally lacking any semblance of hygienic practice; because help was scarce they often changed beds of patients who had not been given fresh linens, but rather were using the soiled bedding of the sick person before them. They went into the poorest of areas and entered homes unlike any they had ever seen.

The roster of volunteers of the Daughters of Charity read like a royal *Who's Who*, with Marie de Gonzague, future queen of Poland; Charlotte de Montmorency, mother of Henry II, third prince of the Condé family (with roots tracing back to the Bourbon family); Madame Fouquet, mother of the

Superintendent; Madame de Lamoignon, wife of the President of Parliament; Madame Séguier, wife of the Grand Chancellor. But soon, the work grew faster than the help; many of these volunteers from the Royal houses needed to spend time with their families and attend to affairs of state, befitting their station in life.

God always forms holy clusters, putting together people He has chosen to do His Will. We can see, with all the diversions placed in our Saint's path, he needed help. Besides, God never wants any of us to think it is we who are responsible for the conversion and healing that comes about, so he chooses others to help us. And so, it was with St. Vincent de Paul. God brought Margaret Naseau into the picture. She had been working on a farm and after milking the cows would teach the illiterate of the farm, the catechism and how to read and write. Hearing of St. Vincent, she set out to join him.

Though she and her lady friends were of good intention, they lacked the necessary direction and leadership to do the work. And so a lady of the nobility, well educated and talented, *Louise de Marillac* comes back into St. Vincent's life. She had known him in Clichy. She had been married a short time when her spouse died. Having heard of St. Vincent and his work with the poor and sick, she left Clichy where she was from, and set out for Paris to meet him. In 1625, she met with St. Vincent and told him her heart's desire was to serve the poor. In 1630, she made a vow to serve the poor, the rest of her life. Serving in the new society of the *"Servants of the Poor"* was all she could think about.

God's Will be done, eight years later, in 1633 Margaret Naseau and her ladies came together in Louise de Marillac's home and the congregation of the Sisters of Charity, also called the Sisters of St. Vincent de Paul was founded.[15]

---

[15]This is the congregation that Catherine Labouré belonged to when Our Lady appeared to her as Our Lady of the Immaculate Conception and asked her to have a medal struck which became the Miraculous Medal.

In 1642, the little company was actively attending the sick, when their beloved Margaret Naseau went to her reward, having contracted the dreaded plague from the sick she so loved. So, she died as she lived, her loins girded, serving the least of God's children, ready to help one more soul, no matter the cost.

The Daughters of Charity continued to multiply. Their beginnings humble, they were now traveling to the whole world, propagating the Faith through acts of mercy, as well as by lessons on the catechism. Wherever you found the sick and suffering, you were sure to find St. Vincent's Daughters, with one mind and heart; caring for the infirmed in hospitals, visiting and serving the poor, mothering orphans, educating young girls, directing soup-kitchens, running dispensaries and homes for the old and infirmed, the mentally ill. Acting as missionaries in distant countries, they have over 40,000 Daughters spread over the face of the earth, today.

The joy and the agony of growing pains

St. Vincent de Paul drew up a Rule which was approved by Pope Urban VIII in 1632, with King Louis XIII giving his added support. The Lord had blessed the Mission so powerfully and quickly that soon the buildings could not hold all the young men seeking to serve the Lord in His royal Priesthood. God's instrument needed help! In 1633, the Lord sent the Prior of the regular canons of St. Victor who, upon hearing of St. Vincent's plight, offered the Priory of St. Lazarus to the new community. Owing to the spaciousness of the Priory, it became the mother house of the Congregation. It had originally housed lepers, but as there was no further need, it would be utilized to house future priests, those who, spreading the Word of God, would bring healing to the leprosy of the soul! This is how the first Fathers of the Mission got the name: *Lazarites or Lazarians.*[16]

---

[16]This community is not composed of order priests but secular priests who take the four vows of poverty, chastity, obedience and stability. They are committed to (1) labor among the poor, feeding their souls as well as their

So great was his work, Pope Alexander VII wrote a brief declaring that all receiving Holy Orders, must first make a ten day retreat under the spiritual direction of the Fathers of St. Vincent's Congregation. In his lifetime, this priest from the most humble of backgrounds, without earthly riches, without high position in society was to touch not only the world of the Seventeenth Century but to continue long after he went to the Father.

It is time to train those who bring the Lord in the Word and in the Holy Eucharist to the faithful.

St. Vincent de Paul could no longer supervise the development of the Daughters of Charity, as his obligation was to the world, not only supplying to the hungry, the bread which feeds the body, but the Bread Who is the Life of the world, Jesus in His Eucharistic Presence. To bring Jesus to the world, that they might know Him and love Him, Father Vincent would need priests! He set about preparing seminarians for the priesthood.

Now they did not have plentiful seminaries like we have, today. Father Vincent used the house of Saint-Lazar for fifteen day retreats, which would prepare young men for the Priesthood, after they had completed their studies of Theology in the Sorbonne. He gave these retreats five times a year. It grew till he was having retreats in all the dioceses of France, then on to other countries and finally Rome.

The seminarians had all of fifteen days to prepare for their ordination to the priesthood, that which makes them priests forever. So, St. Vincent had all his Priests of the Mission speak to their bishops about the problem, and that was the beginning of seminaries and the many years the future priests would study in preparation of so important an apostolate.

✝✝✝

bodies (2) the sanctification of their own souls through spiritual exercises prescribed by their founder St.Vincent de Paul (3) the conversion of sinners and (4) preparing men for the priesthood.

The work of St. Vincent comes to the attention of the King

King Louis XIII heard of St. Vincent and his work. He asked if the Daughters of Charity could be nurses in his armies, and the Priests of the Mission - military chaplains. St. Vincent de Paul and the King became close friends, and the King began to consult St. Vincent. Because of his intervention, the King reconciled with the Queen, Anne of Austria.

February 11, 1638 the King consecrated France to the Blessed Mother and decreed that in memory of that event each year, on August 15th, a procession be made in her honor. The Holy Virgin granted the King his petition; a few weeks after the consecration, the enemy forces that had attacked France retreated! And if that was not enough, as he had prayed for an heir to succeed him to the throne, a son was born, who would be the future King Louis XIV.

In 1643, the King became seriously ill and called for St. Vincent. He prepared his friend, the King, for death. After Father finished chanting the *Te Deum*, King Louis XIII commended his soul to God and the King was dead.

The King was dead; now, as the heir apparent, the little Prince was not quite five years old, his mother the Queen became the Regent of France. She chose St. Vincent to be her Spiritual Director. This was a great honor, and St. Vincent accepted humbly. Under his influence, she changed her frivolous lifestyle and became interested in the plight of her country and the critical crisis attacking her subjects. She sold her jewelry and gave the money to the poor.

The Queen named St. Vincent - Secretary to the *Council of Conscience* (The Congregation of Faith), which in essence is the Grand Council which determines the outcome of all religious matters, settles all questions concerning the Faith and generally resolves everything pertaining to the Church. Since Cardinal Mazarin was the President of the Council, St. Vincent immediately set out, on horseback, for Mazarin's château in Saint-Germain-en-Laye. Now, the Cardinal was one of the most powerful men in France; he knew most of the clergy of France; he was named head of all the dioceses of important Bishops who contributed generously and were great influences on civil as well as church matters. Unfortunately Cardinal Mazarin, not satisfied or secure in his position and power, even as Prime Minister of the Realm, was jealous of the influence St. Vincent had over the Queen.

Every time St. Vincent tried to speak, the Cardinal interrupted him. When he was allowed to speak, the Cardinal mocked him - in front of all the members of the Court! Then the final blow, Mazarin finally ended by ridiculing the poverty of his cassock. St. Vincent responded: *"I am poor, it is true, because all that I have goes to the poor, but I am proper and my cassock is not class, but neither is it torn, nor is it spotted."*

A short while later, Mazarin discharged St. Vincent from the Court and demanded that the Queen cease receiving him. The Queen was torn, for, on one hand, she had confidence in her Prime Minister Mazarin; but on the other hand, she looked upon St. Vincent as a Saint and selfless benefactor to his country. Although she saw in St. Vincent only holiness, and in Mazarin only shrewdness, she made the hard decision to deny St. Vincent de Paul entry to the palace.

St. Vincent de Paul, the Don Bosco of the 17th Century

There is only one God, and St. Vincent made no one on earth God; so although he loved his Queen, he could go on, as his Savior before him, alone, without man's approval or recognition, to do the Father's Will.

St. Vincent, our Apostle of Charity, never lost sight of the poor and never stopped trying to help them rise from their utter desolation. In France, the situation was so dire, mothers were abandoning their babies, leaving them on the steps of churches and convents, and worse on street corners. Then there were those who, out of desperation, sold their babies into slavery, to professional beggars, who would later use the innocent children to soften the hearts of passers-by, so that they would give them money. This deplorable condition came to St. Vincent's attention; he vowed to gather up all the forsaken babies, get back those who were being used as slaves, and provide a home for them. He approached the Daughters of Charity. At first, they were hesitant; this would be a monumental undertaking! But then the Apostle of Love was love itself, and they could not resist St. Vincent or his impassioned cries in the Name of the Baby Jesus, Who was refused a place in the inn.

They gathered all the lost children and gave them food and lodging; they taught them how to read and write, as well as a trade they could work at the rest of their lives. With this ammunition and newly gained confidence they would never be sold into slavery, again. But all this cost great sums of money! The wealthy Daughters of Charity, stripped of their farms and much of their wealth by the many religious wars France had suffered, were about to give up. St. Vincent called an assembly of all the Dames of Charity. He told them that the lives of these children were in their hands; he reminded them that they had had mothers to save them, if need be. Who would save these children; were they, by their exodus condemning them to die? The women burst into tears; they did not have silver but they could sell their jewelry and fine clothes. The Queen donated a château. The Foundling home was solidly established and that worry was behind St. Vincent.

Violence and anarchy bring death to the streets

The greatest festering sore on humanity was the violence which plagued mankind, with no one safe to walk the streets of Paris. Not only thousands of the poor, and unfortunate, but malcontents, professional beggars and vagrants who did not want to work, entrenched themselves on the steps of the churches and in the town square, demanding alms. Occasionally some beggars became thieves and even killers, accosting passers-by in the evening. They became a danger to the citizenry, and the ministers not knowing how to provide for them, had no recourse but to incarcerate them.

Now, St. Vincent had had a similar problem in Mâcon, with the beggars becoming a veritable curse. When they were rounded up and thrown in jail, he was able to secure the release of those who were truly poor and not bandits, and find work for them. But in Paris his course would not be as simple, with her more than 40,000 beggars. St. Vincent began by founding a home!

The Queen donated the grand Hospital of Salpêtrière.[17] The Daughters of Charity organized a work-house. Now, the idea was that the beggars would move into the house and remain voluntarily, without any restraints; but the minister of justice, because of the great number of vagabonds, insisted the whole lot be interred in prison, the truly poor along with the indigents. St. Vincent was very upset about this treatment of the helpless, but he knew all he could do was try to ease the pain and bring some solace to the prisoners by having the Daughters of Charity visit and look after their needs. After he got them released from prison, not all took him up on his generous offer; they had become too dependent on begging and went on with their profession of the street. But when they were in need, they knew they could find a warm welcome in the the houses founded by St. Vincent.

More misery and fire ignite the countryside of France

It seems, when one problem is solved another crops up. Poor *Belle France,*[18] during the Thirty Years War,[19] was laid waste by the pillaging and plundering of her fields and countryside! Soldiers ravaged her once beautiful provinces. No one group - neither French nor foreigners invading France - could take all the blame for what happened. Soldiers, not having received pay for months, were starving and helped themselves to

[17]This building is located near the train station, *La Gare d'Austerlitz.*
[18]beautiful France
[19]read Bob and Penny Lord's book: *Tragedy of the Reformation*

anything in their path. When the peasants tried to stop them from stealing what little they had, they killed the men, raped the women and took the children, leaving behind only the smoke of burning homes, as evidence of their cruelty.

Now there were those who survived. If what they had gone through was not enough, a great famine covered the land. People were desperate; there was nothing to eat. Some searched the fields and the forests for what Mother Nature would yield; they tried to subsist on herbs; they peeled bark from the trees. Hearing of these new victims, St. Vincent organized, poste-haste, a traveling *soup-kitchen*; with this he provided enough nourishment for the peasants to survive, until they could take care of themselves.

There was the caring for the ill and wounded! St. Vincent set up camps with make-shift hospitals in tents, out in the fields. When they ran out of cloth for bandages, they used the fine silks and brocades, donated by the Crown, which had been gowns for special state occasions and fabric used for the grand royal funerals of Richilieu and Louis XIII! The *haves* gladly gave all they had to the *havenots*; although some who write would like to say otherwise. But as we have said before, history is history; this is what the Saints have reported and that's good enough for us.

The Lazarites[20] came, along with doctors and surgeons, armed with medicines for the sick and victims of the epidemic that was spreading across France. They cleared away the bodies of the dead, giving them all proper Christian burials. Those who transported the provisions, had to travel past enemy encampments, risking their lives with each mile, to bring succor to suffering brothers and sisters; but the Priests of the Mission went all the way, from beginning to end, with courage their shield and love their sword. The entire country wrote to St. Vincent thanking him for all he did. They dubbed St. Vincent *"Father of the Country."* St. Vincent truly epitomized the foundation he

---

[20]the other name for the Fathers of the Mission

begun, *"Secours National."*[21] He saved from death or desperation, hundreds of thousands of homeless poor who came to him for help.

Most of the provinces of the North and the East of France benefited from the genius of the charitable St. Vincent. But from 1648 on, there was over the entire region of Paris, dire and desperate consequences resulting from the Civil War, called *"la Fronde"* or the Catapult. And catapult it did, to more and more wars and divisions. This war was primarily between the princes and the parliament, jealous of Mazarin's power. But always, although the battle is among the few, with the few benefiting, it is the people at large, the poor people who suffer.

Although Cardinal Mazarin, now a refugee in Saint-Germaine-en-Laye, had released him from the Court, hearing of the famine in Paris, St. Vincent did not hesitate to render service to the Court, disregarding the apparent danger confronting him enroute. He had to pass the lines of Clichy and thanks to these old parishioners who remembered him, they came to his aid and sent him off with provisions.

Peace at last, but not for all!

Saints and Saint makers. Show me a Saint and I will show you instruments in his or her life who formed their Sainthood whether through love or hatred, jealously or generosity, avarice or selflessness. All these Our Saint Vincent de Paul knew and had in his life.

Going before the Queen, St. Vincent reported the bread had arrived at the capital. A little later, thanks partly to his intervention, a treaty was signed with her adversary Ruell. Peace at last! But the peace was to be short-lived. Once again, Mazarin would make trouble through his deviousness; he convinced the Queen that Condé[22] wanted to dethrone the young Prince, and arrest the young heir to the throne and his friends.

---

[21]*help of the nation*
[22]the one with whom she had reconciled through St. Vincent

She ordered the army to prepare for war! Full of fear, his dirty work complete, Mazarin fled for his life! The Queen manning one of the cannons, gave the command for the gates to be opened! She would greet the unsuspecting Condé when he returned to Paris. He entered the gates, with his men, and because he was innocent, he never expected the reception of cannon balls aimed at him and his troops.

Violence begets violence; the war was on and the people went mad! Incensed by the famine, the wars, the unending loss of lives, the poverty they were enduring, a mob attacked the *Hotel de Ville*,[23] setting it on fire and a senseless massacre ensued with the crowd haphazardly killing everyone in sight.

St. Vincent transformed the Saint-Lazare into a shelter for refugees from the entire countryside. He made provisions for those who were homeless, as a result of the flames sweeping through Paris. But not many came, because not many survived the lunacy that turned the people against themselves.

With courage and fire, but above all with the immense love he had for the poor people, innocent victims of the disputes of the mighty, St. Vincent wrote firmly to the Queen, sharing his thoughts of her and Mazarin. With the throne's interest, primary, the Queen took St. Vincent's advice and the Prince returned *alone* to Paris. He was greeted by cheers and great acclamation, "Long live King Louis XV!" Only he was able to end the war and maintain the peace! One of his first acts was to dismiss Mazarin!

St. Vincent de Paul, Founder and Defender of the Faith

Founder! St. Vincent de Paul founded twenty five houses that stretched to the far corners of Europe from France to Piedmont, Italy, Poland and beyond. Never satisfied, St. Vincent founded other confraternities and called them Charity; they were dedicated to attending the needs of the sick; then another branch of Charity, called *Dames of the Cross* was dedicated to the

---

[23]City Hall

schooling of young girls; and another was created to care for orphan children, most of whom had been abandoned by their parents.

A Priest, forever! Though these corporal acts of mercy were paramount in his mind and heart, he relentlessly pursued his vocation of bringing the Sacrament of Penance to everyone. This Saint cared for the poor and rich equally, the famous and the infamous, Kings and Queens as well as paupers without homes, none more important than that he or she was a child of God. Amidst all the blows, slanders, and controversy which colored his life, this true son of Jesus kept his eyes on the cross; often, especially at the strike of each hour, making the Sign of the Cross on his chest (secretly with his thumb). No matter what happened in his life, good or bad, he always attributed it to the Will of God. Although he longed to be united with His Lord in Heaven, he was sensitive to the suffering of those on earth, and peacefully served them.

Defender of the Faith! St. Vincent never shrunk from telling the truth as he knew it. Now, there was a controversy splitting the Church concerning *"Divine Grace."* Michael Baius was a professor and doctor of Divinity at Louvain, the world renowned university which has been attended by many famous priests like Archbishop Sheen. Baius proposed a theory concerning the Grace bestowed upon man before and after the fall, and other speculations which, among seventy six other hypothesis, were condemned by Pope Pius V in 1567. Baius accepted the Pope's decision and disavowed all that he had written, including his theory on Grace.

Cornelius Jansenius and John Verger, students at Louvain, years later, came up with theories on Divine Grace, based on the errors of Baius that had been condemned. They were so committed to their new theory, Jansenius was convinced to write a book containing his theories on Divine Grace. Later, Jansenius became a Bishop and never published the book. Before his death, he said that he waited upon the judgment of Mother

Church regarding his writings.

But sadly, after Jansenius died his friend Verger had the book published with some embellishments of his own. He became the foremost and most articulate proponent of Jansenism. He was so eloquent that initially even St. Vincent was taken in by him. But when he heard Verger express some of his errors and teach that the Church had failed five or six hundred years before, St. Vincent renounced him and his false brand of Theology. Feeling the weight of responsibility that we all have, to speak the truth and defend the Church against her defectors, St. Vincent used every means at his disposal to expose these errors.

The Sacraments! St. Vincent loved the Sacraments and stressed the importance of all seven Sacraments on the Mystical Body of Christ. He emphasized especially, the *Sacraments of Penance and the Eucharist.* When he taught on confession, he repeated over and over again the importance of making a sincere and perfect confession, being truly sorry for our sins; the danger being those who *pretend* true remorse are more accountable for *this* sin than all the sins they may have eliminated from their confession; for this sin is not only against the Sacrament of Penance, but against the Eucharist, the Body, Blood, Soul and Divinity of Jesus Christ Whom they are receiving unworthily.

St. Vincent de Paul prepares to go Home

At the end, good and worthy father, his thoughts were of those he was leaving behind. It was 1658! Knowing they would need direction after he went to the Father, St. Vincent left each of his sons a small book of rules he had written for them, and pleaded with them to earnestly live by them. His congregation was again affirmed and confirmed by two more popes: Alexander VII and Clement X. Like the other great Saints before him, he gave to the last ounce of his blood. Eighty years old, his body racked with fever, drenched with sweat, awake most of the night, sleep impossible due to his uncontrollable shaking, he awakened, as always, at four in the morning. He did as he had done his sixty years of priesthood; he spent his first three hours praying;

then celebrated Mass; then after Mass prayed for those in the last throes of agony that they might have a peaceful death.

Precious Saint, servant of God, Father Vincent received the last Sacraments, gave his last words of direction to his missionaries gathered around him; then his head gently fell back and he peacefully went to the Lord and His Mother Who I am sure were there waiting to take him home. *Well done, little son. Welcome Home!* On the 27th of September, 1660, after having labored on earth eighty years, he was gone. His congregation buried him in the church of St. Lazarus in Paris, with much ceremony. They all came, those he had touched who had not preceded him Home! They were an amazing bouquet of the Church, all sizes, all colors, nobles and peasants, brothers and sisters, all, filing by his tomb, bidding their friend goodby, for awhile.

Miracles started immediately!

The cause for his Beatification was opened. In 1712, investigating his remains, they found his body beautifully intact, incorrupt. A heavenly aroma rose from the open casket. His clothes were as fresh and unsoiled as the day he had been buried, fifty two years before. The coffin was solemnly closed, and although the people had already proclaimed him a Saint, now all waited for the findings of the Church. Upon carefully, scrupulously going into his life, his writings, investigating miracles attributed to him, Vincent de Paul was declared Blessed in 1729; and in 1742, Pope Clement XII declared him a Saint.

Au revoir, sweet apostle of Charity; we hate to say au revoir

In this dark world where the enemy of God is trying to block out the Light Who is Jesus, where the devil, in his furtive fight to gain men's souls for Gehenna, has deluded everyone into thinking there is no such thing as sin; in this world where people have become amoral, not knowing right from wrong, a voice still cries out, like St. John the Baptist *"Repent and be saved!"*

Like his Savior Who died and had pity for all, even those

crucifying Him, like His Savior Who was born to save mankind, like He Who healed the lame and gave sight to the blind, St. Vincent never sacrificed his Father in Heaven and his vocation on earth, that of a priest of the altar as he served the physical needs of the faithful. He never compromised his love for the Church out of love for the poor and the rich; to him they were all one and the same, loving his God through his neighbor. He was available; no hours too many, no sacrifice too great. Like Jesus, born of the lowest of estates, he came to serve not to be served. Like Jesus he too walked the Way of the Cross, persecuted, abandoned, and humiliated.

There is so much to learn about this Super Saint. To most he is remembered solely for his acts of mercy and charity. But like that other Saint of mercy, Mother Teresa of Calcutta, he was devoted to the Eucharist and the Church, and like her it was the Eucharist Which sustained him in his work and love for the poor. The picture I think we will have forever when we think of this Super Saint is, more than anything else, he was a priest, a true *alter Christus*, another Christ.

Saint of the people

Above: *St. Charles Borromeo*

Above: *As Archbishop of Milan St. Charles Borromeo renounces all his possessions.*

Above: *St. Charles Borromeo held six Provincial Councils and eleven Diocesan Synods.*

Above: *St. Charles Borromeo founds Congregation of Oblates & Diocesan Seminaries.*

Above: *Glory of St. Charles Borromeo in Heaven*

St. Charles Borromeo

Hero of the Counter Reformation

God is so good. He made a promise which He has always kept. He has been a faithful God to a very unfaithful people. We are our own worst enemies, but God always bails us out. We're talking in this instance about the great heretical movement spawned by Martin Luther in the early Sixteenth Century, a pure flame from hell which grew and grew until it exploded into epidemic proportions.

Luther was a victim of his own ego. He was used and abused as a pawn by the powers that ruled Germany during that period. By the time Martin Luther was dying, he had lost all power; the reformation had gotten completely out of his control. Luther had to prepare himself to meet God the Father and explain how and why he left the people of God at the mercy of maniacs and wholesale murderers such as John Calvin in Switzerland, Henry VIII, and in years to come, Oliver Cromwell in England, Scotland, Wales and Ireland. Luther made a statement before he died, "I wanted to get rid of one pope; I created a hundred popes."[1] And it continued to get worse, with all blame being heaped on the shoulders of this dissident Augustinian priest.

We have often said that in times of crisis, God sends us Miracles of the Eucharist, Apparitions of Our Lady, Angelic intercessions and Saints and Other Powerful Men and Women in our Church. This account is about one of those powerful men, a true hero in our Church, Charles Cardinal Borromeo, Defender of the Faith of the Sixteenth Century. He was one of God's soldiers along with Ignatius of Loyola, founder of the Society of Jesus (the Jesuits), Philip Neri and Pope St. Pius V, who went to battle against Luther, Calvin and all the betrayers of the Church; and became heroes of the Counter-Reformation.

---

[1]See *Tragedy of the Reformation* by Bob and Penny Lord- full chapter on Luther and Lutheranism

Luther's massive and potentially devastating attack on the Church of the Sixteenth Century, put the people of God into a tailspin. He was allowed to spew outrageous heresies, encouraged and supported by the greedy governments of the various principalities of Germany who wanted nothing more than to take away the papal lands and not have to pay any royalties to the Pope. They used this man as a puppet, and the world has never healed from the wounds inflicted upon the Church. By the end of the Sixteenth Century, each little principality in Germany had their own religion, custom tailored to the individual needs and idiosyncrasies of their rulers. None of what was given them in the form of doctrine had anything to do with the Catholic Church. But they were forced to accept it. Many Germans, as well as Swiss, Scandinavian and countless other nationalities, were never aware they were no longer Catholic until it was too late.

The Lord was to raise up a brilliant son in Charles Borromeo. He came from good Catholic Italian stock. His father was a Count, very skillful and spiritual. His mother was a Medici, and his uncle on his mother's side was to become Pope Pius IV. So Charles grew up in an aristocratic, truly Catholic background. Charles was born in the castle of Arona on the breathtakingly beautiful Lake Maggiore, one of the most exquisite of the lakes of Italy, north of Milan, bordering the Swiss border. It was the year 1538. Charles was a very serious boy, and sincerely pious. His family played a very instrumental part in matters of the Faith. They were steeped in their religion. Charles could always count on any number of priests or bishops, and even a few cardinals and His Holiness, Pope Pius IV, gracing his parents with their presence. It was in this solid background that he became so strong in the Faith. It was a gift from the Lord which would stay with him all the days of his life.

At age twelve or somewhere in his early teens, Charles was given the Benedictine Abbey of Sts. Gratinian and Felinus in Arona by his uncle, Julius Caesar Borromeo, for his very own.

At that time, he also received the clerical tonsure.² It was interesting how seriously Charles took this gift from his uncle, looking on it as more of a responsibility, than as a means of adding to his personal wealth. As young as he was, he made a point of reminding his father that income from the Abbey could not be used for their household or for any secular purpose, including paying for the upkeep of their palace. He used the income from the property for the maintenance of the Abbey, for his religious education, and for the care of the poor and homeless. Even at this early age, he was very strict and would not use any part of it even for his secular education. He observed the rules beyond the letter of the law. He was very strict, and although in his position, he would have been allowed to bend them, it was not in keeping with his religious beliefs.

In preparation for a career in service to the Church, he learned Latin in Milan. He attended the university of Pavia, where he was taught under the tutelage of Francis Alciati, who later became a cardinal of the Church. Charles had a speech impediment which, coupled with a slowness in grasping the subject material he was given, gave the impression that he was backward. But he was like the tortoise in the account of the tortoise and the hare. He was slow but solid. Everything he learned, he would use to defend the Church of the Sixteenth Century.

The Lord was working on a parallel course. It was 1545, and Pope Paul III called the Council of Trent. It was a brilliant maneuver to accomplish two goals at the same time. He formally condemned the teachings of Martin Luther,³ and defined the

---

²A bishop cut or shaved the front, sides and crown of the head, forming what is called a corona, like St. Anthony wore. This was the introduction to the religious life, and although it was not part of Holy Orders, the surplice was given to the candidate at this time.
³Martin Luther was officially excommunicated by Pope Leo X in 1521, who also condemned 41 of his propositions. But it lacked the necessary power to be accepted by the universal Church because it was not under the cover

doctrines of the Faith. To quote Henry Cardinal Newman, an English convert, *"We do not define dogma until it is attacked."* We can see the Lord gathering up His Army with Charles in Milan, St. Philip Neri in Rome (born 1515), St. Ignatius of Loyola in Spain (born 1491) and the future Pope St. Pius V (born 1504) laboring as a priest in northern Italy at this time, having been ordained in 1528. All these men were born to do great things for Our Lord in defense of the Church.

Getting back to Charles, he was a model student. He fought the label of being slow by being resolute in his commitment to excel in his studies. He showed great strength, imposing upon himself the most stringent demands. Because of his prudent behavior and demeanor, he was held up to the other students as an example of chastity which was badly lacking in the university; he obtained his doctorate in civil and canon law at twenty two years old in 1559.

He exhibited a great deal of control for a young man, his age. His uncle, a Medici Cardinal Archbishop, was elected to the exalted title of Pope Pius IV. He had great plans for his nephew, Charles, making him a Cardinal-Deacon without making him a priest. He also made him administrator of the Archdiocese of Milan, who had no archbishop for some time. Again, this was without being a priest. So Charles was ready to head back to Milan to work for the Church, not as a priest, but as a lay person. However, his uncle, the Pope, had other ideas for this bright twenty two year old future Doctor of the Church; so he brought him down to Rome to work at many marvelous projects His Holiness wanted to accomplish. Knowing that Cardinal Charles was the man for the job, he wanted him near the Vatican. In Charles, the Pope knew he had someone whom he could trust, and who had the reputation in the family of being thorough and *getting the job done*, no matter what it was.

___

of an Ecumenical Council. In 1555, Pope Paul IV convened the Council of Trent to formally condemn Luther and his teachings.

Charles was made legate[4] of Bologna, Romagna and the Marches of Ancona. Then he was named Protector of Portugal, the Low Countries, the Catholic cantons of Switzerland, as well as the orders of the Franciscans, the Carmelites, the Knights of Malta and many others. Charles was becoming a powerful man in the Church and he was still not a priest. He did hold minor orders, however at age twenty three. His slow methodical approach did annoy some people in the Vatican; but there was never cause for concern. The assignments were always executed to the exact degree of excellence of which he was expected to perform, and yet he was never in a hurry to get them done. Everything was customary and systematic. He was never harried. With the death of members of the family, he became in charge of handling family affairs, which he did *again* without getting overwhelmed, and at the same time accomplishing his goals more than satisfactorily.

St. Charles tried as much as possible to liberate himself from all the material trappings connected with holding a position in the Vatican as a legate of the Pope, and yet he felt he was required to live in a certain way, in keeping with his standing in the Church and also his place in his family. But these were traps to him. He wanted nothing to do with them. He committed himself to having a large household and a magnificent palace, befitting his rank and the type of entertainment he was required to put on. He would rather have lived as a recluse in a monastery, with only Our Lord as his companion. That would have been enough for him. Despite the temptations which came his way as a result of his titles and positions, he became more and more disenchanted with this way of life. He maintained mortification in his behavior; temperance and serenity in his demeanor.

---

[4]An officially appointed representative of the Pope. In permanent assignments, he becomes a Nuncio before a civil government, or an apostolic delegate when representing the Pope in affairs of the Church.

We have to believe that St. Charles Borromeo enjoyed being such an intricate part of the workings of the Church, especially being such a holy young man; but he did have one problem which constantly nagged at him. He had been made Administrator of Milan. They had not had an archbishop living in the archdiocese for *eighty years.* And yet he could not go to Milan to dispatch his many duties. I mean, he was in effect, Archbishop of the Archdiocese, which is a full time job, *but couldn't be in his archdiocese to do it.* He was an extremely conscientious young man. He realized he was doing as much as he could handle, but felt that either he be allowed to administer his office on-site, so to speak, or give it to someone else who would be there working with the Church hands-on.

He may or may not have understood that he was a trusted member of the papal team. That word *trusted* is key here. There are not many people that can be arbitrarily trusted to do anything. If someone is a trusted employee, or a trusted member of a church community or government, that person is very special. That trust requires an action. In the case of St. Charles Borromeo and the Pope, that action was complete loyalty to the Pope and whatever he needed Charles to do for him. Charles was a *yes* man. He never gave a thought to not doing whatever was required of him; *but* he was torn between his obedience to the Pope and his obligation to the souls of Milan, which he judged he was not handling as well as could have been handled by someone there full time.

The Lord knew why He wanted St. Charles to be in this key position during this crucial time. It was the Council of Trent. It had been opened *first* in 1545 and adjourned in 1547, without ever having completed the task assigned to its members. Then in 1551, it was convened *again* under a new, determined Pope Julius III, but it was adjourned *again* after one year. The work had never been completed; it had never been brought to conclusion; the reforms, doctrines, none of these things had been instituted. *"The Council of Trent was unquestionably one of the*

most important Councils the Church had ever convened."[5] Until
and unless all the reforms, dogmas, doctrines and declarations
were formalized, the whole Martin Luther controversy was still
up in the air. Until the questions raised by him and his fellow
heretics were answered definitively, their errors clearly
condemned, the dissidents would use this as justification to break
away from Mother Church.

In going through the documents of the Council of Trent, it's
interesting to observe the different attitudes of the popes,
especially the contrast in the Sixteenth session in 1552, in which
Pope Julius III suspended the Council, and the Bull for the
Celebration of the Council of Trent, written by Pope Pius IV in
1560 and the subsequent opening of the Seventeenth session in
1562. Pope Julius III was completely defeated. He had tried to
rekindle the flame which Pope Paul III ignited when he convened
the First Session in 1545. Pope Julius III and his people had
been victims of strong pressure by the German princes.
Protestants had been invited to the Council in the spirit of
reconciliation. But their demands were so ridiculous it was
impossible to concede to them. They insisted that resolutions
that had already been made by the Council, especially those
regarding the Real Presence of Jesus in the Eucharist, and the
doctrine of Transubstantiation should be revised so as to be
based solely on the Protestant interpretation of Scripture, and that
the Pope had to agree to be subordinate to the Council.[6] In
addition, war broke out between France and Germany; the
German bishops left the Council and never returned.

"...(the Council) thus far had arrived only at fragmentary
results: its dogmatic definitions were incomplete, only a fraction

---

[5]Bob and Penny's book: *Treasures of the Church, that which makes us Catholic.*

[6]It is a dogma of the Church that when a Council issues a document
approved by the Pope, the Holy Spirit envelops the Council and prevents it
from making any formal error - *Treasures of the Church Page 163*
It is not the other way round!

of the controversies with the Protestants having been doctrinally resolved; still less satisfactory were its reform decrees, which left unanswered many urgent petitions of the bishops. In 1553, Pope Julius III prepared an extensive reform Bull to cope with the many unresolved practical problems, but he died before it could be published."[7]

When Pope Pius IV, St. Charles' uncle, was elected Pope, he vowed that he would reopen the Council and bring it to conclusion. He had good reason for this. Calvinism was running rampant, not only in Switzerland where Calvin had begun with it, but now it was threatening France.[8]   The Pope's relative, Catherine de Medici, the regent of France, was very weak taking a stand against Calvinism. She vacillated back and forth, almost on a daily basis.

Pope Pius IV knew, through infused knowledge, that he needed a General Council to get the Church at large to support the Council of Trent's stand on Protestantism. He also knew the amount of infighting that would be involved in putting together a Council, whether it be to continue the Council of Trent or convene a new Council. He knew he needed a Charles Borromeo to make it happen. Charles had everything that was needed to get the job done, with two very special qualities, (1) and most important, *loyalty.* The Pope knew his nephew was behind him completely, not so much because they were related, but because Charles supported the Pope's effort to turn the tide of Protestantism, which was becoming stronger and stronger. (2) a quality of sticking-to-it until the job was completed to the glory of God and the Salvation of the Church from her enemies.

It took ten years after the previous council had been adjourned, for the final sessions to be opened. Charles Borromeo had to be in charge of overseeing the Council, so that all obstacles were overcome, in an effort to make it successful. It

---

[7]New Catholic Encyclopedia Vol. 14 - Pg. 274
[8] *Tragedy of the Reformation* by Bob and Penny Lord-chapter on Calvinism

was touch and go many times during the two years he actually sat in on the proceedings. It almost fell apart on a daily basis, bringing back the fear that all the work the Council had been convened for in the first place would never be realized. Charles Borromeo vowed he would not let that happen. God knew he wouldn't. The Pope knew he wouldn't. He just couldn't let anything get in the way of the success of the Lord's work.

Together with the other members of the Council, he pounded out the additional nine sessions needed to put everything into order, to write the dogmatic and disciplinary decrees which were necessary to make the Council a success. It has been attested to that St. Charles Borromeo was the single most important factor behind driving the Council of Trent to its successful conclusion in 1562. The following year, 1563, he was ordained a priest. Within a matter of months, he was ordained bishop. He prayed now that the Council was successfully completed, he would be able to go to Milan and run his archdiocese. In addition to his own feelings about what we could call *absentee management*, that is, bishops of major dioceses and archdioceses living at the papal court in Rome, rather than being among their people, shepherding and pasturing their flock, this had become a very touchy situation during the last two years of the Council of Trent.

But we have to explain Pope Pius IV's thinking, not just his, but all the popes prior to him. Today, we live in a modern world of communications, where nothing happens anywhere in the world that you cannot see and hear about on the six o'clock news. The distances between Rome and many of the Dioceses are not far to our way of thinking, what with planes and cars and Autostrade (Major highways). But in reality for that time, to go to Milan from Rome, for example, which is approximately 572 kilometers, or 358 miles could have been a *two to three week* trip. Communicating was a long drawn-out thing. Even to send a message, it took a horseman about a week minimum, flying like the wind, to get an important message from the Pope to a bishop and vice-versa; and that's assuming the messenger was not ambushed by enemies of the Pope somewhere along the way. The Pope needed the bishops to be there with him, by his side, mostly for loyalty, but also for quick decisions. He had to know they were not plotting against him, running their own little kingdom in their Diocese. Even today, the bishop or archbishop is usually the richest, most influential man in town. He owns a great deal of property, has access to much money, and is the Spiritual Leader of hundreds of thousands of the Faithful. In the case of very large Archdioceses, like Chicago or Los Angeles, the Archbishops of those Archdioceses are Spiritual Leaders to millions of Catholics. What would it take for the evil one to fill a bishop or cardinal's heart with treachery and pride, especially if they were a far distance from headquarters? What would it take for the local prince or emperor to pressure them into disloyalty and disobedience to the Pope? And how long would it take before the Vatican were even aware of a betrayal from one of her cardinals or bishops?

Pope Pius IV was pretty adamant about St. Charles staying at the papal Court in Rome. He did have another reason, however, than just having him available at a moment's notice. The closing of the Council was just the beginning of the work involved. This particular Council, one of the most important, if not *the* most important Council in the history of the Church, had to be followed up with many things. As a supplement to the Council, many works were produced to implement the doctrines and dogmas of the Council. Some of them were:

Revised Index of Forbidden Books was published in 1564.
Roman Catechism for Pastors was published in 1566.
The Reformed Roman Breviary was published in 1568.
The Reformed Roman Missal was published in 1570.

While Charles was not involved in every aspect of these works, he had a hand in all of them. He was particularly involved in the drawing up of the Catechism, and in major liturgical reform, especially where the music was concerned. He actually composed a Mass called "*Papae Marcelli.*" But he felt a great pull to Milan and pressed his uncle to allow him to go there, at least *for a visitation.* Finally, the Pope gave in and allowed him to go, *just for a visitation.*

There had been a vicar whom St. Charles had appointed; he and a group of Jesuits were specifically sent to try to bring about reforms in the archdiocese, and had been mostly *unsuccessful* in accomplishing their goal. It needed the archbishop, whom Charles had become, to go and put things in order, and spend some time with his flock. However, before he left, the Pope appointed him Legate a Latere for all Italy.[9] In effect, St. Charles *was the Pope* in whatever area he would visit during the time he was away from Rome. He had broad powers from the Pope. Again, Pope Pius IV knew to whom he was delegating these powers. St. Charles was his right-hand man.

His time in Milan was well-spent, both for him and the Church. He was able to see first-hand the resolutions of the Council of Trent at work. He taught suffragans[10] at the provincial council he held for the region of Milan. They were instructed in ways to implement decrees such as,
- the discipline and training of the clergy,
- the celebration of Divine Services,
- the administration of the Sacraments,
- the teaching of the Catechism on Sundays.

St. Charles was extremely successful in this provincial council and was sent a letter of congratulations by the Pope. It was during this trip, while he was working his way back to Rome by way of Tuscany, exercising his legatine duties, that he received word that His Holiness, Pope Pius IV, was dying. He rushed back to Rome to be at the bedside of his uncle and friend,

---

[9]Title of a specific, confidential representative of the Pope. Usually, he is entrusted with particular powers to enable him to carry out his mission.

[10]Bishops from other dioceses, sent to Milan to learn from his teachings the reforms of the Council of Trent.

his mentor, his *"Sweet Christ on Earth."*[11]   He stayed with the Pope until he died and his successor, Pope St. Pius V, was elected.

There was no question but that the new Pope had need of the broad experience of St. Charles Borromeo in putting together his papacy. He persuaded Charles to stay in Rome for awhile. But Charles really wanted to return to Milan and his flock. He felt he was just beginning to make breakthroughs with the people of Milan, as well as the priests and bishops of the surrounding areas. But he had given in to the Pope. Remember, it's not that easy to say no to a Pope. I wish the Pope would just ask me something so I could say *Yes!* And this is not just a Pope, but a Pope who was eventually canonized a Saint of our Church. So he had to be pretty special. It probably took all the strength St. Charles had to stick to his guns. But he prayed for perseverance and the right words to explain to His Holiness how important it was for him to return to Milan.

St. Charles enlisted the aid of all the most eloquent saints who had gone before him: St. Anthony, St. Thomas Aquinas, St. Augustine, every Saint he could think of, plus Our Lady and his Guardian Angel as well as the Guardian Angel of Pope St. Pius V. With all that ammunition behind him, he asked the Pope to let him return to his Archdiocese of Milan. He explained how important it was, not only to him, but to the people of the archdiocese, as well as the priests and bishops with whom he had worked. The Holy Spirit worked through St. Charles and whispered into the ears of the Pope St. Pius V. He could understand the importance of this move for St. Charles as well as for the entire Church, and so he dismissed St. Charles with his blessings.

In April of 1566, just a few months after Pope St. Pius V was installed Supreme Pontiff, Charles was allowed to return to

---

[11]St. Catherine of Siena called all Popes. S*ee Saints and Other Powerful Women in the Church*, chapter on St. Catherine of Siena

Milan. This was an important time for him. He had known for a long time how necessary it was for his people to have a full-time bishop. Now he was able to begin working full time for his archdiocese. All the distractions of the papal Court, as beautiful and spiritual as they might be, were taken away from him. There was no longer a need for the big household, or the large staff or the many affairs which he had to put on for the sake of the papal Court. Charles was a very simple person as far as his desires and needs were concerned. He did not want all the wealth which was thrust upon him at various times in his life. Now he could divest himself of whatever was not actually necessary for his subsistence.

His almoner[12] was shocked at the way St. Charles went about giving away as much of his wealth as possible. The first severe task he put upon himself was the tightening up of his household. However, he was never imprudent in the austerity which he practiced. He would never allow himself to become so weak because of his fasting that he would fall behind in the major tasks he had given himself, in the fulfillment of his many duties. So he didn't starve himself. He ate as little as was necessary, just what he needed to do what he had to do. He also had a lot of money. It came from many different sources. But it always came. He didn't need it. He didn't want to accumulate it. So he gave away what he didn't need. He made sure that whatever responsibilities he had were taken care of properly, because that was what he was, a proper person. But he never cared for excess. He was happy to share what he had with those who did not. He was a true Franciscan, even though we don't think he ever became one.

To many, however, his initial move into Milan was considered very radical. He felt that he had *much too much* in

---

[12]A person named by a prince or lord to dispense alms or monies to indigent subjects. In the modern church, that position has been given over to members of a religious community to distribute alms.

the way of possessions. He had to dispose of *a great deal of it* immediately. He sold many things which he owned, of which he held no value. The lion's share of the proceeds from the sale of all this *stuff*, valuable *stuff*, expensive *stuff*, but *stuff* nevertheless, went to the poor, indigents, or what we would call today, street people. As Jesus said in Scripture, *"The poor you will always have with you."*[13] We don't think St. Charles thought that by giving his money away, he could end starvation or poverty. He was a very logical man. He believed in the Scripture passage above. He just didn't need the possessions and knew some people who did need them. So he put his wealth where he thought it would do the most good.

When St. Charles was allowed to return to Milan for good, he found a raggedy archdiocese steeped in abuses and excesses, but more than anything, a flock without a shepherd, longing and hungering for a father figure who would minister to them. They found this in St. Charles Borromeo and more. He was a powerhouse of energy. Perhaps the Lord permitted him to stay in Rome as long as he did to train him for this major undertaking, that of whipping an archdiocese into shape, and making it into a model diocese which would not only benefit the people of Milan and their surrounding areas, reaching as far as Germany, Switzerland and France, but for the whole church. The prototype which Borromeo created has been the standard for the government of physical and spiritual programs within the entire Church until this day.

The people loved him. He was so filled with the Holy Spirit as he spoke to his spiritual children, they could not help but be filled with this love, and project it to whomever they met. It was an epidemic of the most splendid sort. They actually looked forward to persevering in virtue and suffering for the sake of the Kingdom because he made it such a loving way to live. St. Charles so practiced what he preached in his own life that the

---

[13]John 12:8

people wanted to follow him. For instance, his own household was too large, too sophisticated, too cosmopolitan. They lived too well; they shouldn't have; they were mostly clergy. St. Charles wanted to live a simple life; he had to convert his own household. Then he could convert the diocese. And most of that transformation took place as a result of his example rather than his decrees. He had a steep road to climb, and he had to begin with himself. Here is an example of what he walked into:

"Throughout the diocese, religion was little known or understood and religious practices were desecrated by gross abuses and disgraced by superstition. The Sacraments were neglected, for many of the clergy scarcely knew how to administer them, and were lazy, ignorant and debauched; monasteries were full of disorder."[14]

He had to make a clean sweep, build a diocese from scratch, and he did. He instituted so many reforms, it doesn't seem possible that one man could have done it all. And we must keep in mind that at this time, he was only twenty eight years old. It was pure Holy Spirit. He was responsible for the institution of some of the following:

1. Reorganization of Diocesan administration into a workable set of offices with separate, individual functions.
2. He called six different provincial councils and eleven diocesan councils to set policy and a working relationship by the people of the church with each other and with their bishop.
3. He began methodical and frequent visits to every part of his diocese.

   [Author's note: This may not sound like such a big accomplishment to us. Our bishop usually gets to every parish in the diocese at least once every year or so. Keep in mind, however, that this diocese, and most like it at that time, may not have ever seen a bishop in the lifetime of anyone in the parish. This particular diocese, Milan, had

---

[14]Butler's Lives of the Saints, Volume 4, Page 258

not had a bishop living in the diocese for over eighty years. The bishops pretty much stayed in Rome. Plus, even if the bishops wanted to embark on such a grand excursion, their means of transportation were pretty primitive by our standards. If a bishop began a journey to visit all the parishes in his diocese, using a stagecoach, he might never finish it in his lifetime. So you can see what an undertaking St. Charles had given himself.]

4. He opened up seminaries in the Archdiocese, first to the Jesuits, and then to the followers of St. Ambrose.[15] Again, this may not seem like any big thing, but seminaries were not in existence prior to the Council of Trent. Actually, St. Charles was very instrumental in the creation of the seminary system during the Council. So actually, he was basing what he did as Archbishop of Milan on what he was partially responsible for putting into the Canons of the Council of Trent. He so believed in the need for formal education and training of priests that it was one of the first reforms he put into effect in his diocese.

5. CCD - Confraternity of Christian Doctrine - St. Charles created CCD in its original form. Actually, CCD was begun by St. Charles under the inspiration and leadership of Pope Pius IV, his uncle. This was done for the people of Rome. There was such a need for educating the people in the churches of Rome on the teachings of the Catechism that it was begun and promoted in 1560. When St. Charles left Rome after his uncle died in 1565, he brought the concept to Milan and put it into practice, according to the mandate made by Pope Pius IV.

6. He began a diocesan religious society, originally called the Oblates of Milan, which were subsequently named the

---

[15]St. Ambrose was very loved in Milan. He was an early Father of the Church and Archbishop of Milan during very difficult times, leading the people with no thought of his own well-being or comfort. His name and charisma followed him for over a thousand years from the time of his death.

Oblates of St. Charles. This was a reform of clergy which St. Charles began in 1579.

7. He opened up schools and cultural and social institutions within universities in Pavia and at the University of Brera in Milan.

8. He provided shelters for street people of his day: wanderers, the lost and neglected, reformed prostitutes and orphans. Today we would call them the marginalized and disenfranchised, battered women and abused children. The names change with the technology, but the situations remain the same.

We have to stop for a moment to make a comment. Obviously, St. Charles Borromeo was very concerned with social justice. If you just look at some of the reforms for which he was responsible, you know his heart was with his people. He sold and gave away most of his possessions, or at least those that were his to give. He opened up shelters for the poor; he opened up and financed schools. St. Charles was able to accomplish all this without compromising the Faith. This is an important point we have to make here.

He was one of the movers and shakers of the Council of Trent, and the reforms which took place as a result of finalizing the Council. Sweeping reforms were made; not only that but the Council of Trent has been credited down through the ages with being the single *greatest factor* in defining and defending the doctrines of our Faith. But what did the Council of Trent affirm and defend? The Eucharist, the Mass, the Primacy of Peter and our Popes, the Priesthood, the Sacraments, everything that we as a Church profess today, was solidified in the Council of Trent. And St. Charles Borromeo was a leading orchestrator of these reforms. He didn't water down our beliefs. He didn't play down the Faith for the acceptance of a few, or of many for that matter. He didn't decrease the values which have been given to us down through the centuries. And if you look at the reforms he made listed above, he was catering to the same problems in society, which are prevalent in our Church and our world today. And yet he held fast to the values of our Church.

We're told we live in a completely different society today than we did at that time. That's true to a degree. We have more means at our disposal today to relieve the distress of our people. *The problems are all the same.* It is true, today our young people have taken to shooting up schools and schoolmates as well as teachers and parents. It's not unlike what it was then. The big difference today is we've given our people too much access to too many weapons with which will kill! And we've sent them a loud and clear message that life has no value; it's all right to murder. That comes from our legislation against life in all its forms, abortion, assisted suicide and euthanasia. If it's all right for adults to kill, it surely must be all right for children.

St. Charles Borromeo did not feel the need to be popular or liked. You can't put through the kind of sweeping reforms in the Church and the State and have everyone like you. Another advocate of Social Justice of the Nineteenth Century, St. Don Bosco, was definitely not liked by all. He was loved by the children. He was adored by his community. But there were many attempts on his life. The same can be said of St. Charles Borromeo. He was a fighter. He was a Defender of the Faith. Because of the conquests of little principalities by foreign powers, such as dukes of Spain and France, as well as little dictators in Italy, plus inter-marriage for the sake of gaining control of property in key countries, the laws of Milan, just as an example, were completely based on individual agendas.

He found himself at odds with the Spanish governors of Milan over matters of jurisdictional and secular natures. It came to some pretty hard-headed confrontations. In one instance, it was only through the diplomatic resources of the Pope and Prince Philip II of Spain that a sort of peace and arbitration was executed. But then he ran into problems with the clerical communities over the same thing, *jurisdictional and disciplinary authority.* He was actually barred from entering a church by the canons of the Church. When St. Charles would not acquiesce, and persisted in his right to make an Episcopal visit to the Church, soldiers from one of the Spanish dukes, the Duke of Albuquerque, shot at him with a musket. Thank God for the poor aim of the soldier, or the lack of accuracy of the firearms, or the intervention of the Angels, but St. Charles was not hit. However, the Crucifix he was holding was nicked.

In another separate situation, St. Charles was in his home, praying with the members of his household, when a paid assassin shot at him at such a point blank range, it could only have been the wings of the Angels which caused the bullet to graze him slightly. The civil authorities hung the would-be assassin. We're not sure if it was punishment for the crime committed, or for not having successfully concluded the task he had been given and paid to do.

At any rate, it became very obvious to the powers that be, that this was a man to be reckoned with. He was not about to back down from anything, when it came to his Church and his God. Also, his reputation grew outside the diocese of Milan as well. He began making apostolic trips to other dioceses, such as Brescia, Cremona and Bergamo, all to the east of Milan. He made missionary trips into the Italian and German Alps to bring the Word of God to many who were victimized by the widespread lies of *Protestantism*. In addition, in some of these areas which had never had anybody there to minister to them, witchcraft and sorcery were also prevalent. You must remember, this time was when the greatest spread of Calvinism took place. In his travels to Switzerland, he found that although John Calvin had died prior to this time, his heresies were firmly entrenched there. St. Charles took his life in his hands to evangelize there, but he did!

St. Charles Borromeo was considered slow of speech and pace, from what we can gather, however he *ran* his entire life. He burned out at an early age, forty six years old. He was on retreat, when he came down with a fever at the end of October

1584. He was brought back to Milan on a litter. Within three days, he was dead. We believe that he had done all that the Lord wanted him to accomplish in a very short period of time. Twenty six years after his death, in 1610, he was canonized by Pope Paul V.

St. Charles's life was one of great spirituality and dedication to the Church. There were no apparitions of which we're aware, no Stigmata. He was just a solid worker in the Lord's Vineyard. There were many miracles during his lifetime and also which were obviously due to the intercession of St. Charles Borromeo. The most powerful miracles were those of changing men's hearts, of defending the Truths of our Church, and bringing about sweeping reforms in our Church. He was a man of great wealth, who used his riches to benefit those less fortunate than he. He was very focused on bringing the people of God, especially those of his beloved Archdiocese of Milan, back into the fold.

St. Charles Borromeo was a majestic role model, a very special role model, a role model for *Bishops* and *Cardinals*. Everyone needs Role Models! But especially those in authority who have been entrusted by God to shepherd His children. They are answerable; because to the degree that we have been blessed, to that degree we are accountable. Possibly more than anyone, bishops and cardinals need our prayers. Pray to St. Charles Borromeo for his intercession for your bishop or cardinal. He was first and foremost a prelate and Defender of the Church. Now, as a Saint in Heaven, he prays for his fellow bishops who are called to take up his torch and Defend the Faith!

Dear Bishops of the world, your dear brother Bishop and Cardinal didn't give in to the pressures of the day. He *fought* the tensions of his day; if it was not the secular government disputing his jurisdiction, it was the priesthood fighting him over disciplinary actions he was imposing, especially on those complaining that the Church's teaching on Jesus was obsolete in their age. He didn't bring the Church and its marvelous traditions down to the perceived levels of the people. He showed the people how they could rise to the levels of Christ. He didn't allow his clergy to give in to the carnal desires which were so accepted at that time.

Although St. Charles found himself smack in the middle of a church, influenced by the pagan humanism and secular humanism of the Renaissance, he did not capitulate. No, St. Charles brought his clergy to the level of Jesus, in Whose Name they were ministering to the world. The Laity, the street people, the beggars, the marginalized and disenfranchised, were given self worth, *not* by Jesus coming down to their level, *not* by worshipping each other, but by being raised by their bootstraps to the level to which they were called by the Sacrifice of their Redeemer, that of giving His life for them and for us.

We thank you, Lord, for St. Charles Borromeo. Especially in this day and time, when all around us seems so hopeless, thank You for giving us hope. When there seems to be no help, thank You for giving us help through Your servant, St. Charles. St. Charles, pray for us, and for your fellow Bishops and Cardinals.

Above: *Pope Saint Pius V*

Right:
*Statue of Pope Saint Pius V
in the Basilica of
St. Mary Major
Rome, Italy*

Above: *Pope Saint Pius V with the King of Sweden,
Gustavus III on his visit to the Vatican*

Popes of the Counter-Reformation
Descendants of Peter who saved the Church

If there was ever a question that Jesus fulfilled the promise He made to us, *"I will be with you always,"*[1] we have only to delve into the History of the Church, to the periods when we were in dire straits, when it seemed as if the Church, as we have known her, would disappear, be destroyed under the pressure of the enemy. The greatest assurance that we have that Jesus will always be with us is to see how He has *always* been with us. In retrospect, as we read the script He hands us, we would think we were reading a story written for the movies or the stage, everything is so well planned. There is conflict; there is always a conflict. There are major players, unknowns until the Lord puts them into the drama, at which point they become stars of the Communion of Saints. Then He supplies us with a dramatic, suspense-filled story which always ends with us, the good guys, being triumphant. And the best part is the story is always true.

We are endeavoring to present in this book, a series of events and people, the Lord has put together, which gave us the great Counter-Reformation, and those who went nose to nose with the authors of the Protestant Reformation. Watch how the Lord, the great Chess master, puts his players into position, as He needs them to accomplish what has to be done, at this crucial period in history. In the case of the Protestant Reformation, and the major Counter-Reformation which took place within the Church, He placed key people in just the right positions. He took them from unlikely places, then trained them to do the work He had set out for them. They worked together, some knowing it, others not aware of it until all had been accomplished, and sometimes not until they met in Heaven, after it had all been done.

The Council of Trent[2] was a major counter-offensive on

---

[1]Mt 28:20

[2]Read about the Council of Trent and detailed account of the Protestant

the part of the Church, called to condemn and suppress, and hopefully slow down the momentum which was building as the movements begun by Luther and Calvin spread across Europe. There were tremendous intrigues and personal agendas involved in determining why the Council should be formed in the first place; opposition from both ends of the spectrum actually impeded it getting off the ground.

✠✠✠

We want to dedicate this particular chapter to the Popes of the Counter-Reformation, from Pope Leo X, who began the attack against Martin Luther and the Protestant Reformation, to Pope St. Pius V, who finally put into effect all the propositions of the Council of Trent. Again, we want to show you how the most unlikely people were used by the Lord to accomplish the Counter-Reformation. In this way, we know that it was not man in any way, but God who directed the forces to save the Church.

✠✠✠

Pope Leo X (1513-1521)

We begin with Pope Leo X. He was the most unlikely of popes to stand up and condemn Luther and the 95 theses he tacked up on the doors of the Wittenberg Castle on the vigil of All Saints Day, October 31, 1517. The reason that Pope Leo X was the most unlikely person to do something like this was that he was not one who made waves. He was elected because his predecessor, Julius II, had been a very stern Pope. There is a good possibility that this could not have happened during the pontificate of Pope Julius II. He would have sent troops in wherever necessary to quell whatever disturbances were made. He was called the *soldier-pope*.

One of the reasons the young thirty seven year old Giovanni di Medici was chosen Pope so quickly was because he was more interested in the arts, in building a new St. Peter's

Basilica, in protecting the Medici family against her enemies. He was an interim Pope, or so they thought. These interim popes have proven to be the most powerful weapons of the Lord. No one ever thought that he would strike out against anyone. But the princes of Germany and Martin Luther actually aimed their attack against Pope Leo X, blaming him for permitting the granting of indulgences in Germany to those who made donations to the building of St. Peter's Basilica.

And yet when Pope Leo X authorized the granting of indulgences, the normal conditions had to apply. This is that the indulgence is granted provided *(1) Confession and Communion are received within eight days prior or after; (2) the recitation of the Our Father, Hail Mary and Glory Be for the Pope's intentions.* Pope Leo X made these requirements mandatory to receive an Indulgence, no matter how generous the donation was. And prior to this attack on the Pope, Martin Luther had written an extensive thesis on the spiritual value of Indulgences.

Pope Leo X condemned 41 of Luther's heretical propositions on June 15, 1520, and excommunicated him in January of the following year, for which he was later maligned and castigated. This action was so out of character for Pope Leo X and yet the Lord used him to accomplish that goal. He died soon after he did this, at the tender age of forty five. The Church at large would not accept his decision to condemn Luther's heretical propositions because they (the condemnations) were not made under the auspices of an Ecumenical Council. Also, at that time, the Church was not fully aware of the plot against her by the German princes, who were trying to get the papal lands nationalized, and who did not want to pay the papal taxes on the lands.

Pope Hadrian VI (1522-1523)

Pope Leo's successor, Pope Hadrian VI, was the last non-Italian Pope and the first real reforming Pope of the Sixteenth Century. He was from Belgium. He came from the University of

Louvain, where he studied and taught Theology. He was the tutor of the future Emperor Charles V of Belgium; they became close associates. After working with Charles, he went to Spain where he was appointed sole administrator of the kingdom, from the time of Ferdinand V of Castile's death in 1516, until the arrival of Emperor Charles I. He worked as bishop of Tortosa, inquisitor of Aragon, Navarre, Castile and Leon. Eventually, at the request of Emperor Charles, he was made Cardinal of Utrecht on June 1, 1517. But he continued to work in Spain. He was in Spain when news of his being elected Pope came to him. When he arrived at Rome, he had no feeling for the Renaissance, or anything to do with it. He was not that impressed with any of the art. He spent his time trying to get the papacy out of a great deal of debt which was left as a result of the building project of the new St. Peter's Basilica.

He only lived as Pope for twenty months, not long enough to effectively wage the counter-attack on Luther and his heresies that was needed. He started, but he, too, didn't realize what an explosive situation was about to erupt in northern Europe. He did understand that the Church was in need of reform, especially since Pope Leo X had been too easy in matters of spirituality and morals. Pope Hadrian began his reform in Rome, however, it was needed in northern Europe. It was not well received. The members of the Curia had become too used to the good life of the Renaissance. They were not looking forward to sackcloth and ashes.

Finally, he sent an emissary to Germany, a Franciscan, who had been inquisitor in Spain before this mission. He had condemned Luther's teachings in that capacity. But he put a great deal of the blame on the Roman curia for the heresies of Luther. This did not sit too well with Rome. The Franciscan did, however, recommend that Luther should be punished for heresy, and that his teachings be banned, in accordance with the Edict of Worms of 1521. The Edict of Worms condemned the spread of Lutheranism. At the time it was written, it was widely accepted.

But as Lutheranism spread, especially in areas which became prominently Lutheran, the Edict was dissolved.

Pope Hadrian's life was also made difficult by the encroaching presence of the Turks in Europe. They had taken over Belgrade in Yugoslavia, as well as posing a great danger to Hungary and Greece. His predecessor, Pope Leo X, had tried to unite forces in Europe to form a crusade under the Pope, to stop the onslaught of the pagans; but nothing came of it. This new Pope, Hadrian VI, was attempting in earnest to put something together. It could not be easily ascertained which was more of an immediate threat, Lutheranism in northern Europe, or the Turks invading southern Europe. Much of the decision about what to do rested in the Pope's lap. It all proved to be too much for him. He didn't have the strength to battle enemies from all sides. He died after only twenty months in office. But he had begun working on the Counter-Reformation.

✞ ✞ ✞

Pope Clement VII (1523-1534)

The papacy of Pope Clement VII was one of the most unfortunate in the history of the Counter-Reformation. *He virtually did nothing for eleven years.* He was advised by the Emperor, but he chose not to convene a Council. This complete lack of activity in this area dealt a tremendous blow to the Church as Lutheranism flourished, being virtually unchecked for that entire period of time. It spread farther and farther into northern Europe, threatening even Italy from the north. It was a crucial time when action was necessary on our part, and we did nothing.

Pope Clement involved himself in power plays and battles between major European monarchies. Granted, he was in the middle of some very touchy diplomatic situations, having to temper his decisions based on which country was strongest at any given time. He was not, like the ruler of a particular country, able to commit his loyalty to a given power. He was supposed to be the spiritual leader of all these countries, even those who were trying to take over the papal states as well.

Another problem area about which he did nothing was the situation with Henry VIII of England. In 1527, Pope Clement was asked for an annulment by Henry VIII, of his eighteen year marriage to Catherine of Aragon, so that he could marry Ann Boleyn. The Pope sat on it for seven years, hoping it would go away, but it did not. Henry finally took matters into his own hands; he married Ann Boleyn in 1533. By the time Pope Clement VII finally declared that his marriage to Catherine of Aragon was legal on March 23, 1534, the break with England had already become a fact. It was too late. Pope Clement VII died on September 25, 1534.

✟ ✟ ✟

Pope Paul III (1534-1549)

It is a tribute to Our Lord Jesus and the power of the Holy Spirit that Pope Paul III, who in his young years had been full of the shortcomings of the Renaissance, should have had such a major conversion when he was raised to the office of Pope. Again, he was one who surprised everyone. When he was elected Pope, he was sixty seven years old. And while he carried some of his hangovers from the Renaissance, i.e., his great love for art and literature, he also, first hand, realized the need for reform on the part of his cardinals, some of whom were not priests at the time. He realized that if they were going to work for the reform of the Church, they had to leave the outside world *outside!*

Pope Paul III could very well be called the *Father of the Council of Trent.* He was committed to making the condemnations of Pope Leo X of Martin Luther, official for the universal Church. Also, at the beginning of his papacy, the heresies of John Calvin were beginning to surface from Switzerland. By the time Pope Paul III would have been able to begin with the Council of Trent, Calvinism would be in full force. He realized the urgency for a full Ecumenical Council, and he acted on it.

So it was necessary to form the Council quickly, in order to define truths, condemn heresies and hopefully kill this movement before it became any worse, or at least stop the spread of it. When the Pope first decided to convene a Council, there were many questions which had to be answered, such as: *What should be the agenda of the Council? Where should it be held? Should the Protestants be allowed to attend?* All these things had to be resolved, at least in principal, before a Council could be held.

His Holiness tried to convene a Council in Mantova[3] in 1537, but the German and French monarchs blocked their bishops and cardinals from coming, because it was not where they wanted it situated geographically.

It took twenty four years and a great deal of political maneuvering before a site could be chosen for a Council. The choices were Germany, which would not have been good for the Church; and various areas within the Holy Roman Empire, which only existed on paper at this time. Finally, a compromise was chosen - Trent. While it was in Italy, it was at the northern most part, near Austria and Germany. The German Emperor had a great deal of power in this area of Italy, more than the Pope would have wished, so it wasn't the greatest choice from a political standpoint. But the Pope wanted to get the Council convened, and so compromise was the key word. Trent seemed to be the lesser of two evils, and so the Pope accepted it, as did the Emperor; and the Council was begun, at last!

The first convocation took place in 1542 under Pope Paul III, but a war broke out between Francis I of France and Charles V of the Holy Roman Empire (Germany). The turnout was so poor it had to be disbanded in less than a year. However, Pope Paul III was committed to convening the Council; so three years later, on December 13, 1545, the Council officially began in Trent. Two years passed when a Typhus epidemic hit the area.

---

[3]Mantua - near Milan

The Italians blamed the Germans, whom they insisted brought it in from Germany. The Council was transferred to Bologna, and the Council was split again! None of the German and Spanish bishops and cardinals were allowed to accept Bologna, as Emperor Charles V forbid it. Therefore they would not go to Bologna; so the Council was bogged down *again*.

Pope Paul III, wayward youth, but powerful pope, defender of the Council of Trent, died at age 80 on November 10, 1549, two months after the Council had been suspended.

✠ ✠ ✠

Pope Julius III (1550-1555)

It was only by the power of the Holy Spirit that Giovanni Maria Cloche del Monte was elected Pope. We know the Holy Spirit guides us in all things. In this instance, it had to be pure Holy Spirit. There were so many factions fighting so many other factions, which had nothing to do with Church, it seemed like it would never end. It took ten weeks to finally choose a Pope. The French bishops and cardinals were at odds with their German and Spanish brother bishops; because their rulers were at odds with each other. Charles V, ruler of Germany and Spain, in particular, did not like Cardinal del Monte; because he was the main force behind moving the Council out of Trent and into Bologna. But even with all that, after ten weeks, he was elected Pope.

Our new Pope, having come from the trenches, knew that in order to maintain the commitment he and the other Cardinals had made to Pope Paul III, he was going to have to fight against the powers of hell. But he knew that diplomacy would go farther in this quest to get the Council back on its feet than hard-nose tactics. So he compromised his position and started the Council back on May 1, 1551, in Trent. This was not what he wanted, but he had vowed to stand behind the Council, and he did.

So all the work that was done for the two years the Council was held in Bologna was not adopted, although it did set the stage, to work on these areas when the Council was finally transferred back to Trent. However, the Council only lasted about fourteen months and was suspended in April, 1552, due to another political outbreak of war between France and Germany. The situation in northern Italy, Austria, Germany and France became so hot that on April 28, 1552, Pope Julius III had no recourse but to suspend the Council indefinitely. It was not picked up again for *ten years*. And while the official church upheld the condemnation of Luther and his propositions, it was not considered official without the benefit of the Council. For a time, it seemed like the evil one had overcome. But the Lord would not let that happen.

To complete our biography of Pope Julius III, he was devastated by the collapse of the Council. He retired to a palazzo he had built outside the Piazza del Popolo in Rome, and followed the pursuit of the arts, which had held his attention in his youth. He made various appointments, including Michelangelo as chief architect of St. Peter's, Marcello Cervini (the next Pope Marcellus II) librarian to the Vatican. His papacy ended without his having accomplished all he was capable of doing for the Lord. He died of the gout on March 23, 1555.

✟✟✟

Pope Marcellus II (April 9, 1555 - May 1, 1555)

Pope Julius III was succeeded by Marcello Cervini, who took the title of Marcellus II. He only survived as Pope for twenty-two days, so we can't really give him a biography of his own, other than to say his background before becoming Pope gave everyone involved hope that he would revive the reform of the Church. He had his assistants gather together all of Pope Julius III's papers on reform prior to his retirement into seclusion. The thrust of Pope Marcellus in doing this was to write a Papal Bull immediately. But he never got it done. He died too soon.

✟✟✟

Pope Paul IV (1555-1559)

Again, it would seem like the powers raging against the reconvening of the Council of Trent and the Counter-Reformation of the Church, were out working in full force. Pope Paul IV was seventy nine years old when he ascended the papacy. He had no desire to reconvene the Council. He felt that he and a group of cardinals which he would choose, all good men by the way, could handle whatever reform the church needed. He had an obsession with the Inquisition, and as Pope, gave more and more power to the Roman Inquisition. He engaged in unpopular wars, in which he was defeated; and while he hated heresy, the spread of Protestantism reached epidemic proportions. By this time, Calvinism had come upon the scene very strongly, finding its way into Italy from the north. He threatened extreme punishments through the Inquisition against the Protestants, but never did anything to them.

When he died on August 18, 1559, a riot broke out in Rome. The Inquisition Palace, which he had built, was burned down and all the prisoners inside released. They overturned statues of Pope Paul IV, smashing them onto the ground. When his successor, Pope Pius IV assumed the Pontificate of the Church, he had his work cut out for him.

✟ ✟ ✟

Pope Pius IV (1559-1565)

You can easily understand when we tell you that the Lord really had to set up strong fortifications for when the next go-round with the evil one would take place. This Pope vowed to bring the Council of Trent back, and to bring it to conclusion and fruition. Forceful people in key positions, were essential to make the Council work when it finally resumed in 1562. At the beginning, there were so many forces against Pope Pius IV, who spearheaded the continuation of the Council, it seemed as if it would be canceled before it ever got started. He is truly one of the heroes of the Counter-Reformation. We would like to include some of the things he did, during his pontificate, to stamp out the rise of Protestantism which was not only threatening the Church of that day but the Church we have today. This Pope, Pius IV, worked unceasingly for the Council of Trent; if he had not, the Council might never have happened.

To recap what we said before, although the official Church was against everything Martin Luther and now John Calvin were espousing, there were those in the Church who would not accept Pope Paul III's condemnation of Luther's propositions, using the reasoning that the condemnation was not done under the auspices of an Ecumenical Council. Yet these same prelates did everything in their power to defeat and then delay a Council. Their real problem was the pressures they were receiving from the rulers of the countries where their Dioceses were located. That strain was so real that in some instances, their lives were endangered. So it was out of a genuine fear that they acceded to the demands of their rulers.

As a priest and then as Cardinal Giovanni Medici (no relationship to the Florence Medicis) our future Pope Pius IV had a fairly lackluster career. He was more of a diplomat than anything else. But that's what the Lord needed at this point. There had been so much infighting between various countries, that they needed someone who would be acceptable by all countries in order to make the Council a reality. That somebody was Cardinal Medici. The Germans and French both liked him and would accept him. After Pope Paul IV's attack on Spain, Cardinal Giovanni Medici was a breath of fresh air to the Spanish rulers. They liked him. Now remember, none of this had anything to do with the Council. This was just their attitude towards Cardinal Medici as a church official. After the death of Pope Paul V, and after *four months* of convening the college of Cardinals, they could still not agree on a Pope; Cardinal Giovanni Medici was finally nominated; they elected him, immediately as they judged him to be a moderate who would not rock the boat. He was sixty years old. He was a good diplomat. They probably figured, what harm can he do in the next few years? I think they had the same opinion of Pope John XXIII when he was first elected. They called him an *interim Pope.*

However, when Cardinal Giovanni Medici ascended to the Chair of the Papacy as Pope Pius IV, he must have received special graces from the Holy Spirit; and as we're sure that the Pope has special Angels, we believe that they and the Holy Spirit protected him and the Church from error. So while he came out *boldly* and vowed that one of the prime objectives of his papacy would be not only to bring back the Council of Trent, but to bring it to a successful conclusion, he did it with such charm that his adversaries thought it was their idea.

You can see that he was a diplomat. He was also a mover and shaker. Whatever he may have lacked in knowledge about Theology, or the Magisterium of the Church, he gained using the knowledge of people who did know, in particular people like Charles Borromeo, who was his nephew; and although very young at the time, was brilliant. Proof of that is what he accomplished in his lifetime, but in particular with regard to the Council of Trent. Pope Pius IV put Charles in charge of overseeing the Council. But he surrounded him with profound cardinals who would also help to meet the goals of the Council as outlined in 1545 by Pope Paul III, and make them a reality. One of these great minds he chose to use was Cardinal Alessandria, nee[4] Michael Ghisleri, later to be called Pope St. Pius V. *Praise God in all things!*

But we must realize that although Pope Pius IV delegated a great deal of responsibility, he was fully in charge. He was also the driving force behind it. When the sessions threatened to get bogged down because of national or individual differences, Pope Pius switched hats, as was needed. Today, he was the great Pastor, bringing his people out of the darkness of Protestantism. Tomorrow, he was the great diplomat, smoothing ruffled feathers of fellow bishops from countries where the rulers had their own

---

[4]another word for born

agendas. He also calmed the rulers themselves. And as we said, they liked him, so they gave him latitudes they would not have given his predecessor.

This dear Pope had barely six years to get the job done. If he ever had the slightest desire to relax his insistence that the Council move forward, he was prompted by a new offensive being launched by Calvinists into Italy and France. He worked with the heads of those countries. He actually even donated money to the rulers, especially of France, to wage wars on the Huguenots.

It was during his time that Elizabeth I of England began her rule. Actually, she became queen in 1588, after her half-sister Mary Tudor, died on November 17 of that year. This was the year before Pope Pius IV took office. Elizabeth was dead against Rome and the Catholic Church. Pope Pius IV hesitated to formally excommunicate her in the hopes that she might return to the Church. She had been Catholic during the reign of Mary Tudor, but that was in name only. While she kept many of the Catholic traditions, she put the nail in the coffin of the Church the year after she assumed the monarchy by creating the Acts of Supremacy and Uniformity in 1589. The Pope waited and hoped.

By 1563, Pope Pius IV had completed his work on the Council of Trent. He dissolved it on December 4 of that year, and then confirmed the decrees orally on January 26, 1564, and followed it up with the formal Bull of acceptance, *Benedictus Deus* on June 30, 1564. Now that part of the job done, he had to go to work to get the world to accept the decrees of the Council of Trent. He began immediately in Italy; but it was an uphill battle which he was not able to bring to successful conclusion during his lifetime. He began working on the new Catechism and a reform of the Missal and Breviary.

Can you see how he worked along the same patterns our Pope John Paul II has followed, trying to implement the decrees of Vatican Council II, not according to the "spirit of the Council," but *according to the decrees* of the Council. None of this was completed during his lifetime, but providentially, his nephew, Cardinal Charles Borromeo would get the job done. In keeping with his God-given ability to get the right people to do the right job, Pope Pius IV gathered together a commission of Cardinals which later became a congregation, to interpret and enforce the Council decrees. He may not have had the theological background to do the job himself, but he knew people skills enough to get the right people to do the job. Pope Pius IV died on December 9, 1565. Through him, the Lord had accomplished in less than six years what had not been done in the prior forty years. *The doctrines had been defined; the heresies and heretics had been formally condemned.*

Pope St. Pius V (1566-1572)

The work of the Council continues!

We oftentimes think the Lord doesn't let one or two people do everything in Salvation History, because then there would be nothing for us to do except follow what has been passed down to us. The Lord wants us to feel a part of things. Well, here we have the next Pope taking the torch, so to speak, from his predecessor, and running with it. It was crucial that the right man be chosen, who could take the work of Pope Pius IV, and bring it to conclusion. All the work of the years before, since 1521, would be culminated in not only the decrees of the Council, but even more difficult, having those decrees implemented and enforced. It would take a strong man to do that. The man whom the Lord chose to continue the work of the Counter-Reformation was a brilliant man who was able to be molded into a Saint. He became St. Pius V.

Pope St. Pius V, was born Michael Ghisleri in a little village in the Diocese of Tortona near Alessandria[5] in northern Italy in 1504. He was a firm believer in the Truths of the Church.

---

[5]This area of Italy has brought us many holy people, including Don Bosco, Dominic Savio, Aloysius Gonzaga and Pope St. Pius V.

He embraced the Dominican Order at age fourteen and entered the Seminary. From the beginning of his days in formation, it was obvious to all his superiors that he was chosen far above the rest. The Dominicans knew he would go far in the Order, do great things for God and advance the rule of his Father-in-Faith, St. Dominic Guzman.[6] He did move ahead as his superiors thought he would, assuming the posts of lector in Theology and Philosophy for many years. He also served as novice master and in the governing houses of the Order. He did well as a Dominican. St. Dominic would have been extremely proud of him. He was sent to the Dominican convent in Pavia, near Torino. He was for many years second only to the provincial of the Dominican order in Italy. In 1550, he was given a difficult task, that of inquisitor at Como, which borders Switzerland. At that time, it was a hotbed of Calvinist insurgents. His methods of operation caused him to cross swords with the bishop's vicar-general, who thought he enjoyed his job a bit too much. However, it also brought him to the attention of Cardinal Carafa, who would later become Pope Paul IV. Now Cardinal Carafa was a member of the Inquisition in Rome. His philosophy was akin to that of Ghisleri, the young priest from Como. At a time when enemies were more plentiful than friends, he embraced the young priest. He saw in him firmness of purpose and purity of faith. He was Church; and he projected Church to all he met.

As the Dominicans had seen his potential, so had the rest of the Church, especially Cardinal Carafa. After he was elected Pope, he consecrated Michael Ghisleri Bishop of Sutri and Nepi in 1556 at fifty two years old. A year later, Ghisleri was given the title of Cardinal. He took the name Cardinal Alessandrino, after his city. While this was a great honor, it also took him away from the Dominican Order where his heart was, because his duties had to be now focused on the dioceses of which he was in charge. He was a very humble man, and would rather have

---

[6]Read about St. Dominic in Book I of this series, *Journey to Sainthood.*

spent his time praying and writing prayers to be used by others, whom he judged more capable of bringing the Church into the last half of the Sixteenth Century, without losing any more brothers and sisters to the Protestants.

Keep in mind what some of his concerns were. His diocese was just south of the Swiss border. Calvin had made enormous strides in Switzerland, and was sweeping into Italy from the north. France was on the west, not that far away. The French Calvinists, who were called Huguenots, were more vicious in their attacks on Catholics than Calvin, if that's possible. No, that's not possible. No one was worse than Calvin, with the possible exception of Elizabeth I[7] of England, illegitimate daughter of Henry VIII and Ann Boleyn. But as a Cardinal and Bishop, you can understand his concerns for the Church at large, and his diocese in particular, being right smack in the middle of the problem, and being the head of the Inquisition for the Italian provinces on the Swiss border. Remember, he was a Dominican. Dominicans had been in charge of the Inquisition all over Europe from the time of St. Dominic. It was an honor, surely, but it was also a major task.

To add more burdens to his job, he was made Grand Inquisitor for life. Cardinal Alessandrino was not someone who would go quietly in the night. To the contrary, he was a bold, solid person when it came to the rights and wrongs of his Church. And he didn't care if he ruffled the feathers of Popes, which he did, or rulers of countries, which he also did. He found himself the recipient of many criticisms from Pope Paul IV, who had been his mentor, his kindred spirit, on more than one occasion. Then when the new Pope Pius IV, the diplomat, came into power, he was again rebuked. You must understand that he was not a diplomat! He was not on good terms with monarchs who were allowing heretical groups to breathe down his neck from

---

[7]As Pope Pius V, he would excommunicate Elizabeth I of England on February 25, 1570.

two fronts, France and Switzerland. Also, Cardinal Alessandrino would not back down from the Truths of the Church, especially in his position as Grand Inquisitor, even if it meant upsetting one of these monarchs, or, unfortunately at times, even his Pope. By the time Pope Pius IV died in 1565, relations between him and Cardinal Alessandrino were strained, to say the least.

There was even a point in his career when he just wanted to give up his various jobs and go back to his bishopric in Piedmont to live out the end of his career in peace. He had a problem getting back to Piedmont, however, when he took ill and had to recuperate in Rome. Again, this was another area of contention between the Pope and many of his bishops and cardinals. Even the Pope's nephew, St. Charles Borromeo was against it. Cardinal Alessandrino was against bishops living in Rome, which he made no bones about, but which estranged him from the Pope.

We know it has to be pure Holy Spirit that Cardinal Alessandrino was unanimously elected Pope in only nineteen days after the death of Pius IV. More ironic is that the major force promoting him for Pope was Cardinal Charles Borromeo, nephew of the Pope (Pius IV) with whom Cardinal Alessandrino had so much trouble. St. Charles recognized in Cardinal Alessandrino the strength which would be needed, not only to bring the Church through the problems with the Protestant Reformation, but the Moslem dilemma, which we haven't even addressed yet. St. Charles also was given infused knowledge that this man would be able to get the Council of Trent back on track and brought to its conclusion. He was right on all counts. On January 7, 1566, he began his Pontificate as Pope Pius V. The world would know him as Pope *Saint* Pius V a hundred and fifty years later.

Bishops had to go back to their Dioceses
　　　　One of the greatest gifts Pope Pius V gave to the people of God was ordering the bishops of the Church to return to their dioceses and take up permanent residences there. As we

mentioned, this had been a bone of contention with other Popes, especially Pope Pius IV. There had been problems in the past when communications from the Pope to various bishops would be delivered incorrectly, or would get to the attention of a bishop too late for action in certain instances. Then there was the problem of bishops running little dynasties of their own. All of this was counter-productive to trying to run a *universal* Church. But during the time of Charles Borromeo, a system of papal legates[8] was established. These people were representatives of the Pope who roamed around, from Rome to their designated dioceses, instructing the bishops on different rules and instructions which the Pope wanted carried out.

There was a very bonafide reason for the bishops to get back to their dioceses. The people were without a spiritual leader. They had their priests, but they were only to take care of a particular parish and its needs. They needed the pastoral care of a father figure who would tie in all the aspects of a given geographical area, as well as spiritual area. They needed a person to tell the pastor of this parish to get his act straight, while congratulating the pastor and flock of another given parish for building the people of God according to the laws of the Church. Prior to this time, dioceses were administered by what we would call *absentee management*. The boss was not there. The bishop is the head of a given portion of land which is his diocese, and he should be there to take care of his people. In the Archdiocese of Milan, before this rule was put into effect, they had not had a resident bishop for *eighty years*. That's too much time for a flock to be without a pastor, more than two generations.

Pope St. Pius V instituted wide sweeping reforms within the Church. He felt that there were unjust and inappropriate practices going on. The first area of reform he brought about was right in the papal palace. According to his Dominican standards, it had become too opulent. He instituted an austere way of

[8]a Papal Nuncio

living, which did not affect the way in which outside guests were treated, but for the Pope and his immediate entourage, he insisted they be religious first, and nobility, if necessary, second. That went over well with some, and not so good with most. However, he stuck to his commitment.

He wrote broad legislation, for the Church at large, dealing with everything from outlawing prostitution to forbidding bull-fighting. The expanse was outstanding. He was accused of trying to turn Rome into a monastery. His response was that Rome could use a little purging. He practiced what he preached. He fasted and abstained more than he asked of anyone else. He was personally a very holy man, proof of which is he is a Saint, canonized by the Church. He used personal money to import food into Rome, to give to the poor people during time of famine. He took the corporal works of mercy to heart. He visited the sick, the prisoners and the dying. He ministered to them as the Dominican Friar that he was. But on the other hand, he was very stern with matters of the Church. He did a review of religious orders, closing some down, and admonishing corruption in the others. He adopted in Rome and for the whole Church, some of the reforms which Cardinal Borromeo was carrying out in Milan and other parts of northern Italy. One of these was the need of seminaries for prospective priests. Pope Pius V opened seminaries in various parts of the Catholic world.

Being a Dominican and Pope had its drawbacks. Traditionally, the Dominicans had been given dominion over the Inquisition. That was from the time of St. Dominic. Everyone was waiting for him to re-institute the Roman Inquisition, which had been dormant for some years. During the pontificate of St. Pius V, it was again encouraged. But the Roman Inquisition, actually the Inquisition as a tool of the Church, was nothing like the Inquisition in Spain. In Spain, it was run by the government, with the permission of the Holy See. It was intended to root out converts in name only, of Jewish and Moorish beliefs, who were trying to take Catholics away from the Church by teaching against the Faith. It was not a group of fanatics running amuck, completely out of control.

You must keep in mind that the people of Spain, in particular, had been ruled by Moslem forces for over 700 years. The Moslems of that time, also known as Moors (in this instance, as they were so dark), were brutal invaders, who tortured, and killed Catholics who did not give up their Faith in favor of Islam. When the Catholic Queen and King, Isabella and Ferdinand, reconquered the country in 1492, they wanted to bring the Faith back into Spain officially. They demanded that any Jews or Moslems who had converted in name only, but were not truly converted, leave the country.

There were abuses, as there were abuses in the Roman Inquisition. Laws were broken; some punishments meted out of proportion to the crime. But by and large, the Pope used the Inquisition as a means of keeping dissident or heretical clergy in line. You have to remember the period of time we're in. This was the height of the Protestant Reformation. In addition to Lutheranism, you had Calvinism, and the French Huguenots, plus just plain monarchies who were trying to destroy the Church.

Pope Pius V was attempting to hold onto his priests, his bishops, his flock. The poison of heresy upon heresy was spewed from the mouths of Lutherans on one side, Calvinists on the other, and anyone else who had a questionable philosophy they wanted to impose on the Church and the people of God. There had to be some control over what was being taught in the churches, schools, and seminaries.

A great aid to Pope St. Pius V in stemming the tide of Protestantism in all its forms in the Church of the Sixteenth Century was the publication of many works which were produced to implement the doctrines and dogmas of the Council of Trent. Some of them were:

A revised Index of Forbidden Books
A Roman Catechism for Pastors
The Reformed Roman Breviary

The Reformed Roman Missal

The Catechism in particular, was a powerful tool against the errors of Protestantism. We find the same things happening today. Our Pope, John Paul II's Catechism for the Catholic Church, which explains simply the teachings of the Church, has helped many Catholics who would otherwise have been victims of irresponsible theologians or adult education teachers, dispersing material which was heretical. Some of this was done intentionally, to confuse and take Catholics away from the Church. Some was done by people who just wanted to preach a different gospel from the one Jesus taught us. Their intent may not have been separative, but the results would have been the same.

The English Problem

Pope St. Pius V may not have been the greatest diplomat, but he was a solid priest, whose main goal was to hold onto the sheep who were in his flock, and bring back those who had left the flock. He felt a great responsibility to try to bring back England to the Catholic Church. Henry was dead. Whatever happened was over. Let's pick up the pieces and reconcile. Henry's illegitimate daughter, Elizabeth I,[9] had successfully ascended the throne of England after some frightening times. She did not trust many people, and no one in the Catholic Church. There were overtures to her to come back to the Church, but these were translated as means for the Spanish monarch to take over her country.

We must remember that the first great insult to Spain was Elizabeth's father, Henry VIII, claiming that his marriage to Catherine of Aragon, a strong Spaniard, was illegal. Spain also had ulterior motives in wanting to expand their kingdom. So it was a combination of loyalty to the Pope, revenge for the outrage

---

[9]Born out of wedlock to Henry and Ann Boleyn, his mistress. The Church upheld the marriage of Henry and Catherine of Aragon, making Elizabeth illegitimate.

committed against Catherine of Aragon, a member of their royal family, and a desire to expand their colonies which influenced the minds of the monarchy of Spain. To the Spanish monarch's mentality, Elizabeth was never accepted as queen of England, because she was the daughter of Henry VIII and Queen Catherine's lady-in-waiting, Ann Boleyn.

The Pope really didn't want to get involved in what was a very sticky situation which his predecessors didn't want to touch. Reality had to tell him that at this point, Elizabeth was in power in England. She had weathered many storms, and looked like she would remain queen until her kingdom could be forcibly seized or her natural death. But she was queen at this time, and the Pope had to concern himself with the millions of English Catholics who were being denied their rights of religion. It's not said just how much diplomacy was attempted to reconcile the Church with Elizabeth. She may never even have known about many attempts which might have been made to bring England back into the fold. Her advisers had their own agenda, and for the most part, they were happy to be free from the Catholic Church in Rome.

At any rate, Pope Pius V tried to invoke his God-given right to being above secular monarchs, especially in matters of the Church. After all diplomatic means were exhausted, and under pressure from Catholic monarchs, Pope Pius V issued a Papal Bull in 1570, excommunicating Elizabeth I and absolving the English people from obedience to her, and forbidding them to accept her as monarch. Well, you know how the English feel about their royalty, right or wrong. The Bull made the situation between the Church and Elizabeth worse than it had been, if that was possible. The rank and file Catholics in England loved their queen; they didn't want her to be Pope, but they were loyal to the throne anyway. They were caught in the middle.

Loyal British Catholics had a major problem, because at this point, in retribution the Oath of Allegiance, which had not been enforced to any great degree prior to this time, became a weapon to force Catholics to either give up their religion, or be branded traitors to England and to the queen. The Church lost a lot of people in England and less in Ireland when this happened. But it did determine that the Catholic Church in England was defunct. What Martin Luther and John Calvin could not accomplish in Europe, Henry VIII and his followers accomplished in the British Isles.

The Threat from the Other Side of the World

We're not going to attempt to say that the pontificate of Pope St. Pius V was the most difficult in the history of the Church. There have been many at least as difficult or possibly more difficult. But suffice it to say he had a monumental task to accomplish for the Lord, in the six years he held the reins of the Church. His problems never ran in sequence, one following upon the heels of another. That might have been too easy to handle. Rather, they always ran concurrently, everything coming at him at the same time from different directions. Isn't that always the way when you're working for the Lord.

In the midst of the problems he was encountering, doing battle with the Protestants, and especially Elizabeth of England, he was also called upon to defend the Church from the other side of the world, the militant spread of the Moslem Turks. This was another situation his predecessor let fester, hoping it would go away. This plague had been going on for centuries. Europe had closed its eyes when the Turks, under the leadership of Ottoman and his disciples, had been taking over more and more of Asia and North Africa. Then they came into Spain in the Eighth Century, spreading into France, as far north as almost reaching the city of Tours.

It had begun with Sultan Ottoman Mohammed II. Following the success of his father in faith and mentor, Mohammed I, who had enjoyed great success by uniting his people and forming the Arab states in the Seventh Century, the Ottomans grouped together little principalities which had been overrun by the Mongols. Although it began loosely, at the end of the Thirteenth Century, and over the next two hundred years, it gathered tremendous strength, eventually taking over all of the Near East, North African principalities of Syria, Egypt, Tripoli and Tunisia. They were able to be successful in their campaign to make great strides in Europe for two simple reasons. They were becoming more and more united, adding small emirates into their Arab kingdom as they advanced, which attributed to their strength. On the other hand, the Europeans were becoming more separative, fighting with each other over everything, wasting all their resources at a time when they should have been uniting against a common enemy. Their focus was turned inward and towards themselves, and they didn't realize they were being swallowed up from the South.

After Constantinople was captured by the Turks in 1453, which effectively ended the Eastern Roman Empire and opened up the Balkan states and Hungary to the onslaught of the Turks, they began working their way over to Italy. This still did not get the attention of the Europeans, in particular the Italians, until the island of Cyprus was jeopardized. The rich merchants in Venice earned much of their income from Cyprus as a port city. That was one of the reasons the Turks wanted it. The ruling powers in Venice attempted to maintain their control of Cyprus diplomatically, by being friendly with the Turks. (Sounds a lot like how the whole world reacted to Hitler in the 1930's.) They thought it worked, because they didn't know that their enemies were shrewder than they. It was only when the Sultan, Selim II demanded the surrender of Cyprus that the Venetians realized that they had not been very cunning. They were in trouble and did the natural thing; they went running to the Pope.

Pope St. Pius V was aware of what had been happening at the hands of the Moslems. He also realized that if they were able to, they would successfully put all Italians, nay, all Catholics, under the heels of the unbelievers, as they had the Spaniards for seven hundred years. But with all his other problems all over the world, he, as the rest of Europe had done, put the situation with the Turks on the back burner until he could get some of these other problems resolved. But now the Venetians had come to him for *immediate aid.* They were afraid their island port would be taken away from them by the Turks, and knew that was just the beginning. They recalled how Yugoslavia had been taken over.

A campaign was designed to meet the Turks on the field of battle in Greece, across from the south of Italy. It was best to try to stop the invasion before it got close to their own shores. All the ruling royal houses committed certain amounts of military equipment, including ships, guns, bows and arrows, and whatever type of weapons of war might have been used at that time. Actually, it was a means of uniting these separate powers, if only for this one battle. Spain would pay one-half, Venice one-third, and the Pope would pay one-sixth of the cost. Of the total number of ships sent, Venice provided 108, Naples 29, Genoa 14, Spain 13, the Pope 12 and Malta 3. Don Juan of Austria, half-brother of Philip II of Spain, was chosen as the leader of the operation. Everything had been put into place for an offensive at the beginning of October in 1571.

They gathered at the coast of Messina, on the tip of Sicily. Their advance scouts returned from the area where the Turks were stationed. They advised the heads of the fighting expedition and the Papal Delegation representing His Holiness, Pope Pius V, that they were greatly outnumbered. On the foremast of the main ship being controlled by Don Juan of Austria, a banner bearing the image of Our Lady of Guadalupe was placed. (She had appeared to Juan Diego only forty years before in Mexico, in 1531.) The Pope had word sent to all the people in Sicily, as well as throughout the entire Catholic world to begin a Rosary Crusade. The only way the Catholics could be victorious over the Turks was through prayer.

From Messina, the Christian ships sailed down the Greek coast and crossed the Gulf of Lepanto, near the tip of Ithaca.

There they discovered the enemy. When the Christian troops estimated their opponent's strength, it concurred with the information they had received at Messina. They were heavily outnumbered. However, with Our Lady at the helm of the ship, being represented by the banner of Guadalupe, this grossly undermanned remnant of His Holiness was victorious over the enemy. The Turks fled from the area, sustaining a loss of over 30,000 men and a great deal of ships. It was here that the onward thrust of the Moslems was effectively stopped. It was done through the prayers of the people of God and the intercession of Our Mother, Our Lady of Guadalupe. It is said that all during the campaign, Pope Pius V prayed, at times in an attitude similar to Moses on the mountain, with his hands raised towards Heaven. He called for fasting and rosaries to be prayed in all the churches in Rome and wherever the word could be spread. At the Church of Santa Maria sopra Minerva in Rome, petitions were pouring out during the heat of the battle. It is said that Pope St. Pius V was in the middle of a business meeting at a crucial point in the battle, which was taking place some five hundred miles away. At a point he stopped, went to the windows of the Vatican, opened them and listened for a time, as if in ecstasy. Then he turned with tears in his eyes and a smile on his face. He spoke to those with whom he was holding his meeting. He said to them, *"This is not a moment to talk business; let us give thanks to God for the Victory He has granted to the arms of the Christians."*[10]

In honor of Our Lady's aid in winning this battle, the Feast of Our Lady of Victory was instituted by Pope St. Pius V. The feast day is October 7. In recent years, the name of the Feast has been changed to Our Lady of the Rosary, but held on the same day. In addition, he placed the invocation, "Our Lady, Help of Christians" into the Litany of Our Lady.

---

[10]Butler's Lives of the Saints - Pg 236

Who was this Pope, and why is he a Saint?

Pope St. Pius V was a man of God, truly a man of prayer, a holy man. While this is not to say the other popes were not men of prayer, the difference here is that he depended solely on prayer. His ongoing philosophy was, God would move men's hearts; men would not move men's hearts. Pope Pius V brought his Dominican way of life into the Papacy. He brought spirituality back into the office. Again, this is in no way a criticism of any of the Popes who have lived, especially those who were so influenced by the world of Renaissance, in which Pope St. Pius V was smack in the middle. But unlike many of his predecessors, he was not a Renaissance Pope. He didn't care about paintings or buildings, or works of art.

One of his great accomplishments as Pope was raising St. Thomas Aquinas to Doctor of the Church in 1568.[11] St. Thomas was the first Saint given that distinction after the early Church Fathers. Prior to this, the last Doctor of the Church was St. John Chrysostom. All of these Doctors' titles had been given before 750 A.D. Pope St. Pius V was so impressed with the works of the *Angelic Doctor*, as St. Thomas was called, that in addition to declaring him Doctor of the Church, he sponsored a seventeen volume set of the complete works of Thomas Aquinas, which were recommended to be used in all seminaries.

There were those who criticized Pope St. Pius V for trying to turn Rome into a monastery. That was an exaggeration, of course, but the truth lay somewhere in between. Rome was in need of reform. He was trying to refocus this, his city, the city of the Church, back to where it should have been, facing God. Keep in mind that this dear man had so many strikes against him. He had the Protestants from one end, the Moslems from another end, and he ruled in the midst of the Renaissance, one of the most

---

[11]Doctor of the Church - a title conferred on eminent ecclesiastical writers because of their learning and holiness of life; they are always canonized. Their writings are used in seminaries to teach the Faith.

ungodly periods in the history of the world and of the Church. Happily, through all the complaining about how Rome had to change and reflect more its major inhabitant, the Church of Jesus Christ and His main representative, *"sweet Christ on earth,"*[12] there were many compliments on how the attitude of Romans had changed during the brief pontificate of St. Pius V. For that short time, it did become the *Holy City*. A point of interest might be the fact that the white clothes the Popes wear in these modern times comes from St. Pius V, who, upon ascending the throne of the Papacy, donned the white vestment of the Dominican Order, and had it modified to suit his station as Pope.

His background had been the Inquisition. As we mentioned previously, this Inquisition was not the same as that of Spain, which had begun after the Catholic Kings had finally taken their country back from the Moslems. This office of the Inquisition was to deal with Lutherans, Calvinists and Huguenots in France, Germany and Switzerland, who were pouring over the borders into Italy to bring their heresies to the people of God in this country. It was not easy to control dissidents and stem the tide of heresy, which was rampant all over Europe when he assumed office.

The office of the Inquisition of Italy was more recently called the *Holy Office*, and is now called the *Congregation for the Doctrine of the Faith*, and is chaired by Cardinal Ratzinger. The Roman office of the Inquisition was begun by Pope Paul III in 1542, just when Protestantism and Calvinism were sweeping the north of Europe. He had good reason to weed out heretics, and to put the fear of God into would-be-heretics. Granted, at the beginning, the methods of the Inquisition were anything but democratic. A rumor or a whispered accusation was enough to bring someone before this autonomous group of people. There

---

[12]what St. Catherine of Siena called our Popes - for more on this powerful Doctor of the Church, read Bob and Penny Lord's book: *Saints and other Powerful Women in the Church*.

was virtually no defense allowed, no confronting of accusers. It was an extreme form of backlash against those who would destroy the Church.

When Pope St. Pius V was a Dominican priest, he had been made an inquisitor by Pope Paul V and then by Pope Pius IV. There had been an Inquisitor's Palace in Rome before he began his pontificate. It was destroyed after the death of Pope Paul IV by an angry mob. There were those who believed that the Inquisition had outlived its usefulness; it was old-fashioned for these times of enlightenment, this period of Renaissance. And so it had never been rebuilt. But to an old war-horse like Pope St. Pius V, who had eventually been given the title of Inquisitor for life, it was a very necessary means of combating the enemy. So, he brought it back into full effect. Only God can be the judge as to its excesses. It was able to discourage many who would feel the freedom to take pot-shots at the official Church, and engage in heretical activities.

From the time of Pope St. Pius V, the office of Inquisition, now the Congregation for the Doctrine of the Faith, has always had Dominicans (Watchdogs of God) in key positions. This has always been justified by the fact that the first Inquisition was carried out under the supervision of St. Dominic. In an effort to balance the books, so to speak, members of the Friars Minor have also been included as part of the Office. The Church has always exercised temperance in the operation of this office. The prayer has always been that justice is tempered with mercy, controlled by the Holy Spirit.

Pope St. Pius V died the year after the victory of Lepanto, on May 1, 1572. He was very loved by the people. He had not been with them that long as Pope, only six years. He had received a great vote of confidence after the Battle of Lepanto. He was mourned deeply by the populace of Rome. His body was transferred from St. Peter's Basilica to the Basilica of Santa Maria Maggiore in Rome. He was buried in a special chapel and a statue of him sits on top of his tomb.

He did not win the friendship of many of the European rulers during his papacy. He had a difficult situation to handle on many fronts and was not able to resort to diplomacy very much. When the situation called for tact, he tried to use it. He was not trying to win popularity contests, but he did not want to afford himself the luxury of being cold to an adversary when benevolence and compassion would have accomplished the desired result. He was a good man, a bull in a china shop, but he was God's man. To quote from one of his biographers,

"Behind the image of stern lawgiver, of a new Moses, which he projected, lay kindness, and zeal for the well-being of the Church. Besides guarding it against heresy and the might of Islam, he encouraged its expansion through the missions, and was a patron of learning, especially the ecclesiastical sciences. He was not indifferent to the arts, but thought of them principally as secondary to religion. Thus he left only a modest impression on the architecture of Rome." [13]

In effect, he didn't leave any monuments in stone which outlived him. He was not looking for a tribute to his name on earth, but rather in Heaven.

He was beatified one hundred years to the day after his death, on May 1, 1672, and was subsequently canonized forty years later on May 22, 1712. History has told the story of this strong man, totally committed to his God, to his Church, and to the people of God. He was tried and found to be a powerful soldier of the Counter-Reformation. He did what he could to stem the tide of Protestantism in the only way he knew how. And the Church has honored and rewarded him by raising him to the Communion of Saints. No greater reward can be given to a man of God. We thank You, Lord Jesus, for giving us this great Defender of the Faith at a time when we needed him desperately. Lord, we think You've given us a Pope St. Pius V today in Pope John Paul II. Please give him strength and health. We need him.

---

[13] New Catholic Encyclopedia Vol 11 - Pages 396-398

St. Robert Bellarmine

Cardinal, Doctor of the Church,
Father of the Counter-Reformation

St. Robert Bellarmine, brilliant follower of St. Ignatius of Loyola, has been credited with being one of the most outspoken critics of the heresies of Martin Luther and John Calvin. He focused the Church of his time on the true teachings of the Catholic Faith, which were contradicted by the Protestant Reformation. He is one of the powerful men in this book which the Lord sent to construct a suit of Spiritual Armor to defend His Church in this crucial time of crisis. He was so brilliant that the Pope would not, could not allow him to retire to a small Jesuit novitiate of Sant'Andrea towards the end of his life. He was too needed. The Holy See was not ready yet for him to back off from his defense of the Church. He was put in our midst in our great hour of need, and he fought valiantly to defend and protect the people of God.

St. Robert was born in the picturesque mountain town of Montepulciano of noble parents, Vincenzo Bellarmino and Cynthia Cervini, who was Pope Marcellus II's half sister. He was sent down from Heaven on the Feast of St. Francis of Assisi, October 4, 1542. The family was noble, but they were poor all their lives. The Lord had great plans for Roberto. He would not allow his mind to be cluttered up with desires for material possessions, so from the very beginning of his life, He kept these temptations away from our future powerful man in the Church.

His parents knew he was specially gifted by the Lord from the time he was an infant. There was a feeling teachers could tell as soon as he entered into school that this boy had the makings of a brilliant man. They watched his progress, as he grew up in the Lord and in his studies. His preferences always leaned towards the religious life; so it was not a great surprise to his parents when he expressed a desire to join the Society of Jesus, the Jesuits, when they opened a school in Montepulciano.

Remember, the Society of Jesus was only officially canonically accepted by Rome two years before he was born. So this was a new order in the Church. They were exciting. Ignatius, the founder, was active in the Society of Jesus until Roberto was fourteen years old. So when he asked to transfer to the Jesuit school in his town, everyone believed he wanted to be part of the excitement Jesus was creating with this new community of men. For their part, his professors and parish priests could see the potential of Robert. At an early age, he had mastered the masters - he knew Virgil by heart; he could play instruments; he held his own in public debate. When he reached seventeen years old, the Jesuits wanted him; they could see how great an asset he would be to the Society of Jesus. They said of him: "He is the best of our school, and not far from the Kingdom of Heaven."[1]

Robert was so in love with all he was a part of at the school, he wanted to join the Jesuit order as a brother. His father was dead against it. But he had a friend and ally in his mother. Who can refuse a mother, especially when she is as persuasive as Cynthia Cervini. Plus she had some influence with the Pope, who had influence with Vincenzo and so his father gave in and wrote to the general of the order, Fr. James Laynez, asking him to consider his son for their order in Rome. Fr. Laynez was one of the original members of the Society of Jesus. In 1537, on July 25, with St. Ignatius and Fr. Faber, he went to the ruins of an old abandoned monastery in Vicenza, and together they officially formed the Society of Jesus.

Reading in between the lines, Fr. Laynez must have had communication with the superior in the school in Montepulciano, and received superlative reports about Robert Bellarmine. They wanted Robert in the Jesuit community. But Father Laynez consented to Robert's father's terms that they wait one year before Robert enter the Jesuits in the event he should change his mind. However, when that year was up, on September 15, 1560,

---

[1]Butler's Lives of the Saints - Vol II Pg 293

Robert was on his way to Rome like a shot, and his new life in the Society of Jesus. He immediately went to the General's quarters where he made his religious vows.

He stayed at the mother house at the Gesú for a short indoctrination period, after which he was sent to the Roman College to begin his studies. During that time, he was able to mingle with the brothers of the Jesuit fellowship and acquaint himself with the lifestyle of the Society of Jesus. He found everything they did, to his liking. Actually, he loved everything about the Jesuits. Another special gift about spending this short time at the mother house, was to be able to walk through the rooms which had comprised the residence of the founder of the order; Ignatius of Loyola, had not yet been canonized a Saint (he was only dead four years in 1560). Robert was enthralled to be able to touch the things that Father Ignatius touched. It was a special experience for the young brother.

His instructors at the Roman College could see in short order, what a brilliant and highly spiritual candidate they had in Robert Bellarmine. They gave him special attention during his three years at the Roman College, and as soon as he had finished his Philosophy courses, they sent him to Florence to teach. They had ulterior motives, however. He was not well. They felt that the climate near his home of Montepulciano, only a day's distance from Florence, could bring his health back so he could continue on with his studies. The following year, he seemed strong enough to send him to Piedmont, to teach.

There was a little catch in his situation in Mondovi, in Piedmont. He was supposed to be teaching his students Cicero and Demosthenes. But Demosthenes was not Latin; he was Greek. Robert didn't know any Greek. A man of lesser stature would have gone crying to his superiors, *"How can I teach them the writings of a Greek philosopher, when I don't know any Greek?"* Instead, he decided that if he was going to be teaching, he had better learn Greek. So, the night before he was to teach, he studied the grammar lesson that he was to give in Greek, the following day. In that way, in short order, he conquered the Greek language.

He began to preach in the local cathedral. His sermons were so powerful that people would come just to hear what the Lord was saying through this young Jesuit. So stimulating were his remarks that he became the talk of Mondovi. Naturally, his popularity came to the attention of his local provincial, who sent him to Padua to study Theology. What can we say about Robert? Was he a quick study, or was he Divinely inspired? We'd like to think that he was Divinely inspired, given Infused Knowledge, which he would use to glorify God by combating the heretical teachings which were taking root even here in Italy. He was sent to Padua to prepare for ordination. They really didn't want to take chances with superlative minds like Robert Bellarmine. They always lived with the fear that the secular world might attract him, or worse yet, the Protestants would. They were trying to take any good minds away from the Catholic Church. So Father Adorno, his provincial in Piedmont, was wise in his thinking.

But in Padua, the same thing happened, only on a grander scale. While he was studying Theology, *and* preparing for the priesthood, or as part of preparing for the priesthood, he was asked to preach every Sunday at the Cathedral in Padua. Again, he became one of the favorite preachers in Padua. Now, Padua is somewhat different from Mondovi in Piedmont. Without casting aspersion on the mental faculties of the people of Mondovi, Padua has always been the home of the most brilliant minds of Europe. Padua and Bologna were at that time, the greatest University cities in Europe, Padua number one, and Bologna, number two. To get better than that, or on an equal par, you had to go to Salamanca, Spain, where St. Ignatius, the Father-in-Faith of Robert Bellarmine, studied.

Before Robert could finish his studies in Padua, he came to the attention of the father General, St. Francis Borgia, who was on a par with Ignatius himself. He had become Father General in

1565 when Fr. Laynez died. He inherited the Protestant Reformation in full swing. He saw in Robert Bellarmine, a potent force against those who were proclaiming Protestantism all over Europe. So in less than two years in Padua, he was sent, without having been ordained, to the University in Louvain, Belgium to get his degree in Theology. Now, Louvain has always been ranked with the great universities in Europe, only as a Catholic university. It specialized in studies of the Catholic Church only, and to this day, is considered a Catholic University.

Robert was asked by Father Borgia to focus his preaching to the undergraduates on a vein combating the heretical teachings of Michael Baius, who was the chancellor of the University of Louvain at the time. He was teaching erroneously on many subjects, including but not limited to Original Sin, Fallen man, Redemption, Justification and Merit and Papal authority. Baius' teachings had been condemned by Pope Pius V twice, in addition to having been censured by many universities and varied seats of learning, including the University of Paris and Cologne. It was a good direction in which to point Robert Bellarmine. We wonder if St. Francis Borgia knew at the time, he did this what the far-reaching effects this would have on St. Robert Bellarmine and Counter-Reformation Theology. It was a brilliant move, if not Divinely inspired. His preaching against Baius was but an introduction to teach against all those who were denying the Truths of the Church; and remember, this is during the raging hotbed of the Protestant Reformation. Luther had only died in 1546; Henry VIII the year after in 1547; Calvin had only died in 1564, five years before this time, so their errors were being spread more rapidly than Baius. That was where the urgency lay.

Robert Bellarmine had an urgency to enter the priesthood, but had to obey his superiors, and what they considered priorities. However, the Lord finally whispered into the ears of the responsible parties and Robert Bellarmine was ordained in Ghent, Belgium in 1570, on the Feast of the Annunciation. He continued working at Louvain because there was a great need for his spirituality first, and his great knowledge second. And when the Jesuits opened their own school of Theology at Louvain the same year, Robert Bellarmine was made the first professor of Theology in the school. He proved that he was a man without an ego, devoted to furthering the Truths of the Church. Rather than attempt to come up with some teachings of the modern school of Theology, he taught Theology based on the writings of St. Thomas Aquinas. This was a brilliant decision, because he could not go wrong with advancing the teachings of one of the most brilliant minds of the Church. And while Robert did not point a finger at Baius or Calvin or Luther or Henry VIII in either an intellectual or spiritual vein, he succeeded in contradicting their philosophys with the works of a brilliant peer of his, one whose authority could not be questioned - Thomas Aquinas!

He stayed here for seven years. During that time, he did some of his most important work. He was a brilliant homilist. Though he was not tall, and not really good-looking, he had such an aura about him that the people flocked to hear him speak. They said his face actually glowed when he spoke in defense of the Church and for the Glory of God. For Robert Bellarmine was speaking the Word of the Lord. He had to stand on a stool, but that didn't keep the crowds from coming, and more importantly, from listening.

Another extremely important work which was begun during his tenure at Louvain was a book entitled, *Controversies.* It was a short, concise, but very powerful apologetic on all the teachings of the Church in response to all the attacks from the Protestants. The full thrust was to defend the Church against the attacks of the Reformers. Most of it was based on study of Scripture, Church History and Patristics.[2] It was a simple book, but covered all aspects of our Faith belief in the areas which were being disputed. It was the basis for a much larger work he did in

---

[2]Writings of the Early Fathers of the Church - i.e., Augustine, Cyril of Jerusalem, Ignatius of Antioch and etc.

later years. But this compact textbook was so well done and so informative, priests began carrying it around in their pockets as a reference guide to use on the altar during Masses, or when they found themselves needing to defend the Faith. *Controversies* became so popular that both Catholics and Protestants (who wanted to understand the truth of the Catholic Church) read it.

The University of Louvain became the front-line for defenses against heresies. It was also the think-tank where the great minds of the Church were sent to formulate resistance measures against the enemy. It was an exciting opportunity the Lord gave Robert Bellarmine, but as will be seen shortly, it was more for the Church and God's army than it was for Robert that he spent these seven years in residence at Louvain.

In 1576, the Pope felt it was necessary to bring Robert back to Rome. He had been trained long enough. He knew how to instill the teachings of the Church into young students. Now it was time to do the same for the seminarians and priests in the *Eternal City.* He was put in charge of teaching "controversial theology" at the Roman College to English and German missionary students. Why would you think English and German students, and why on earth, missionary. We have but to look at the times. This is the midst of the Protestant Reformation in Germany. It is also forty years after Henry VIII began his attack on the Church of Rome. We had been weakened badly in both countries. We needed men with good solid theological background, to be missionaries in those countries. Many of them were to become Martyrs for the Faith as well. Controversial theology dealt with those theological controversies that were causing such division in the Church, mostly at this point, with the church of England and Germany.

Robert Bellarmine worked tirelessly in the field of Reform theology and an active member of the Counter-Reformation for the next fourteen years in the Roman College. Actually, he worked against the Reform for the rest of his life, which is why he, along with the other powerful men of the Church in this book were given the title of Saints of the Counter-Reformation. Due to his unrelenting teaching, preaching and debating, many came back to the Catholic Church. His arguments were too logical and too elegant to be anything other than dictated by the Holy Spirit.

Papal Power

By its very name, you have to know that this was a very touchy subject. As a natural outpouring of the Protestant Reformation, Luther immediately attacked Papal power. He maintained that all power emanated from God, and that it funneled down through the princes of the various countries, especially Germany. Their power was superior to ecclesiastical authority. He and the princes of Germany, who were supporting him in every way, had ulterior motives. They did not like the idea of their country being ruled by Italian powers.

Calvin originally supported separation of Church and State powers until he found himself in the position of possessing both powers. He was able to make the smooth transition from church leader as a minister in Geneva to the dictatorial head of the state. Being a brilliant deceiver, he was able to mislead the people and heads of the state by making the proclamation that the function of civil government was to be simply the preservation of the law. He demanded that the enforcement of religion and personal piety be based on his doctrines. Now here's where he double talked his case. It was unlawful and immoral to be against the state unless the state violated God's Will as defined by Calvin. However, with all of that, he maintained that the Pope had no temporal power in Switzerland, or actually, wherever Calvin was able to proselytize.

Henry VIII picked up on both of these philosophies when they suited his purpose. He maintained that he was the spiritual leader of Britain, and that his laws superseded any other leader. Therefore the Pope of Rome had no jurisdiction of any kind in England. Even the Archbishop of Canterbury, who became in effect, the Patriarch, or English Pope, was subject to the throne.

In France, the situation reached crisis proportions when

Gallicanism was adopted. This gave the ruler of a country complete control over the Church, even to the point of appointing bishops, subject to only an offhanded, informal approval by the Pope, which approval could not be denied. The prelates they appointed may not have been in the best interests of the Church.

The situation was getting completely out of hand, with temporal rulers trying to maintain *temporal* and *spiritual* power over their countries. The Pope needed help! It came from Robert Bellarmine. He upheld the papal spiritual supremacy, but drew the line when it came to the Pope's temporal power. To his way of thinking, the Pope was a spiritual leader, not a king or secular ruler of a country. He maintained that the only time the Pope could exercise temporal power was when a monarch threatened not to execute laws which would protect the Church's rights in their country, or to unseat a sovereign who was heretical.

This caused more trouble for Robert Bellarmine than it meant to solve. He put himself on bad footing with the papacy, who did not want any limitations put on papal power. The Pope felt that more than enough restraints were weakening papal power throughout Europe. He needed a strong, solid stand in this area. Robert Bellarmine was more obedient than anything else. He, as a Jesuit, gave over complete loyalty to the Pope. He changed his position, accepting that of another brilliant Jesuit of the day, Francisco Suarez, who agreed with Bellarmine about the spiritual power of the Pope, but maintained that the papacy had the right to interfere in a country's religious policy because princes were subject to Divine law, which superseded civil law. Robert Bellarmine came out of this situation basically unscathed, but with the spread of Protestantism and basic anti-clericalism in various countries, the Pope's power steadily weakened over the centuries.

However, the greatest death-knell to papal power came, not from outside the Church, but as is always the case, from within. The first blow was a theory called *Febronianism*, which was penned by a German bishop under a pen-name, Febronius. It maintained that the Pope had illegally taken power and therefore had no more power than any bishops. Not only that, but no decrees, neither by a pope, or a council, had any legality in a country unless the ruler approved it. This was conveniently picked up by most German monarchs, and when an Austrian cleric adopted the same philosophy under the name Josephinism, it was a defeating blow to our dear Popes.

In 1598, Robert published a Catechism, which also became an immediate success. It was translated into sixty two languages, and was still being used as late as the Nineteenth Century. You see, all of Bellarmine's works were extremely popular. Why do you think that is? He spoke Jesus. He gave the people the Truth. He was more accepted than all those theologians, who were coming out with *"new"* forms of theology. Robert Bellarmine used Scripture, Thomas Aquinas and the Magisterium of the Church. There was no secret.

When we give Parish Missions, at times priests complain the donations are plummeting. We ask them if they give them Jesus. *"If you bring them Jesus,"* we tell them, *"you'll never have problems with collections. You'll get as much money as you need. Only do what you're here to do."* That's what Robert Bellarmine did, he gave them Jesus.

Robert Bellarmine, Cardinal Archbishop

In 1599, Robert Bellarmine was made a cardinal of the Church and a few years later, in 1602, he was consecrated Bishop of Capua, which is just north of Naples. We're not sure what the thinking was in putting him out to pasture, so to speak. For our Saint, however, it was an opportunity to do something he had not really been able to do in all his priesthood, shepherd his flock. He spent his time in Capua as a true pastor, focusing on charity and reform. But it was common knowledge among the powers that be in Rome that there was much more for Robert Bellarmine to do than spend the rest of his days in a small diocese in southern Italy. That was soon to become apparent in the actions of the new Pope, Paul V. He called him back to Rome in 1605 to serve as a Defender of the Faith. At Pope Paul V's request, he took over such offices as the Holy Office, (Ratzinger today) the Congregation of Holy Rites, the Propagation of the Faith, and many other important posts.

Robert Bellarmine, Don Quixote of the Reformation

Robert spent the rest of his life defending the Church. He truly rode his trusty steed against the windmills, the dragons, the powers of hell of his time. He was a hero in the true sense of the word, willing to give up his own life to preserve the values of his Church. He did whatever it took. There were times when he thought he would not come out of a situation unscathed. But he had the promise of the Lord, and he fought with his last ounce of courage, to dream the impossible dream.

Robert Bellarmine plunged into sticky situations *"where angels feared to tread"* where no one else was willing to take a stand, risk a reputation or a career. He cared not for rank nor reputation. He had already accomplished whatever fame the Lord wanted him to have. He only used his name to advance the teachings of the Church, and to defend her against her enemies, who were within and without. Most of his enemies could not stand up against his brilliance and expertise in the fields of Counter-Reformation. *He actually invented Counter-Reformation.* When Cardinal Bellarmine entered into a situation, it was obvious to all concerned that he would deal with it from a true Church perspective. He was fair, but in the final analysis, he was Church. He was also a winner.

The Pope chose Robert because he had no fear, going up against kings, nobility and the famous of his time from any country. He fought against Gallicanism in its French form and as it spread to its English equivalency, as well. He countered the claim of King James I of England about the *"divine right of kings"* and the English Oath of Allegiance. You must remember that all of this was taking place after England began to enforce her Act of Supremacy (1534) and Oath of Allegiance (1606) by torturing and killing her subjects in England, Scotland and Wales, and of course, in Ireland as well. In addition to these battles, he continued to defend the papacy against those who would deny the *temporal authority* of the Pope.

There is something we have to consider when talking about Robert Bellarmine and his role in the Counter-Reformation of the Church. He took a lot of criticism for standing up for the Church. He had a lot more courage than many others in his position at that time. But the thing we have to realize is that he had come up against a situation which the Church had never experienced before. There were not rule books to tell him how to behave in a given situation. He wrote the rule book as he went along. If you recall, when he first went to the Catholic University of Louvain, and the Jesuits had opened their school of Theology, that was the beginning of what was termed Controversial Theology. It had not existed before Martin Luther and Calvin and Henry VIII began firing broad sides at the church. No one knew what to do. It was during his time that counter-attacks to the offensives being hauled at them were formulated.

Another thing we must consider is that as a Jesuit, and a good Jesuit at that, his main goal was to protect the Pope. This was the vow that Ignatius of Loyola had taken in the name of all Jesuits at the very beginning, and Robert Bellarmine was committed to keeping that vow. Popes had vacilated over the meaning and limitations of papal power before Robert Bellarmine came out with a definitive statement on it. No matter what the Popes may have said prior to the time he made his statement, whatever the present Pope, Pope Sixtus V, felt was in the best interests of the Church, Robert Bellarmine had to support. And he did, with his life and reputation.

Robert Bellarmine was a very spiritual priest. Although he spent most of his time in duties regarding teachings of the Church, he never allowed himself to stray from his spiritual life. He made at least one retreat a year, at the beginning only eight days, but as he became more mature in the Lord, he extended these retreats to thirty days. It was obvious that Robert was trying to separate himself from things of the world, even the world of the Church, and concentrate on things of the soul. During his retreats, he wrote beautiful spiritual books, entitled *On the Ascent of the Mind to God*, (1614) *The Eternal Happiness of the Saints*, (1615) and *The Art of Dying Well* (1620). As in the case of all his books, they became popular immediately and are considered special spiritual reading to this day.

One of Robert's greatest problems was that he was in such demand. As he got older, he desired to get back to his Jesuit roots. As a young Jesuit, he had not anticipated the type of work he would be doing for the glory of God. He most likely thought he would go to any one of a number of missions all over the world, and teach and preach. Now that he was approaching eighty years old, he felt he would like to go back to a Jesuit novitiate anywhere but preferably out of the light of the public eye, which he had occupied for most of his life.

But he was too valuable to the Pope. He could not be allowed to retire. Even after Pope Paul V died in 1621 (the same year that Robert Bellarmine died), he asked the new Pope, Gregory XV if he could be allowed to retire. He was really getting old and his hearing was bad. This Pope told him he could not be spared; he was needed. And Robert said *yes*, a weak and tired *yes*, but a *yes* none-the-less. However, the Pope did allow him to move into the Jesuit novitiate where he had longed to relocate for many years. But his joy was short-lived. He moved in on August 25, 1621; and three days later, he was attacked by a violent fever; and died within three weeks - on September 17, 1621.

When it was obvious to all that he was on death's door, His Holiness came to visit Robert Bellarmine, whom all considered a living Saint. His brother Cardinals surrounded him and signed him the way Cardinals do. They put their skullcaps and crosses on his chest, and prayed for his intercession when he arrived in Heaven. There was no doubt in anyone's mind that he would be there very soon.

Robert Bellarmine was a very humble priest. He asked for a very simple funeral, but the Pope felt it would have been an injustice not only to the memory of Cardinal Bellarmine, who had been such an important part of the Church of the Sixteenth and Seventeenth Centuries, but to those who would aspire to do the kind of work that Robert Bellarmine had given his life to do. Our Pope knew that Bellarmine had to be willing to give up this one luxury, that of an inconspicuous funeral, for the possibility of inspiring another Robert Bellarmine who might be in school at this time, or in the Seminary, or not even born. Saints beget Saints. Our dear Pope knew that. He knew the Church would need another St. Robert Bellarmine; he just didn't know how soon.

Robert Bellarmine had another request, a simple petition. It was given to him, but it took three hundred years for him to have it fulfilled. He had been very close to St. Aloysius Gonzaga,[3] a young Jesuit who died prematurely in 1591, when St. Robert Bellarmine was on sabbatical from the Roman College. He had kept in touch with all the students at the Roman College, of which Aloysius Gonzaga was one. Aloysius was a particularly special student, with whom Robert would speak at length about the Kingdom of God, and things of a spiritual nature. He became Aloysius' Spiritual Director. He was with Aloysisus when the young Saint contracted the plague from a patient at Our Lady of Consolation hospital in Rome. He had lifted the sick man out of his bed, which he should not have done, and contracted the dreaded disease. He was put to bed at the Roman College on March 3, 1591. Robert stayed with him the entire time of his infirmity. Aloysius was a frail, weak boy. He never recovered from the illness. He died three months later, on

---

[3]Read about St. Aloysius Gonzaga in book II of this Trilogy, *Holy Innocence, the Young and the Saintly*

June 21, 1591. While it's not known for sure, it is believed that Robert Bellarmine was with him on the night he died. Aloysius was buried in the church of St. Ignazio in Rome. Robert asked to be buried at the feet of the young Saint. However, because of the prestige of Cardinal Bellarmine, it was fitting that he be buried in a place of more prestige. He was buried in the official Jesuit church, the Gesú, in the Chapel of Our Lady. But on May 13, 1923, on the occasion of his Beatification, his body was removed and transferred to the Church of St. Ignazio. He is buried next to St. Aloysius Gonzaga. Praise God!

St. Ignatius of Loyola

Above: *St. Ignatius is Miraculously healed by St. Peter.*

Above: *St. Ignatius of Loyola prays at a cave in Manresa, Spain.*

Above: *St. Ignatius decides to become a Soldier for Christ.*

Above: *St. Ignatius of Loyola and his companions take their first vows.*

Above: *Our Lady with St. Ignatius of Loyola*

Saint Ignatius of Loyola

Soldier, Poet, Mystic, Author, Defender of the Faith
and Founder of the Society of Jesus

Saint Ignatius was born in 1491, the year before Christopher Columbus was commissioned by King Ferdinand and Queen Isabella to go to the New World, in thanksgiving for Spain having been liberated from the yoke of the Saracens. For nearly 700 years, Spaniards could not worship in Catholic Churches; they were deprived from receiving the Sacraments; religious and clergy were exiled, imprisoned or killed; all mention of Jesus was forbidden under the penalty of death. How did the people from whom our Saint comes, preserve their faith with this persecution going on for most of seven centuries? How did Spain and the Catholic Church raise up such powerful soldiers as the much maligned Catholic Queen Isabella, Saints like Teresa of Avila, John of the Cross, Paschal Baylon and Ignatius of Loyola to mention a few? We believe the answer lies in the stories of Saints and Martyrs, and others not yet proclaimed.

Spain had survived this scourge of physical and spiritual domination which had covered her plains from North to South and East to West; it was a time for rejoicing and thanksgiving. What they did not know was that another attack would be leveled at this faithful nation of Saints, a new attempt to destroy the Church which Jesus founded. But God, all-Omnipotent, He Who is, was and always will be, He Who is beyond time and space, He Who sees all and knows all, and upon knowing all, does all to save His Church, raised up a powerful army of Defenders of the Faith, to save this faithful nation and others which would fall under another type of tyranny.

As the *enemy* of God's holy Church is raising up men who would bring about a revolution called the Reformation, God is calling forth soldiers to counteract this revolt, an army which will bring about a *true* Reformation, a *Counter-Reformation*. This is the story of one such Saint!

A child is born who will change the course of history!
History brings us to the part of Spain, known as the Basque country, to the Castle of Loyola in Guipuzocoa. A child is born; Ignatius (baptized Ignio) was of noble blood, his family from a long line of nobles. His father was Don Bertram Tañez, lord of Oñaz and Loyola and head of one of the oldest families of Spain. The lineage of his mother Doña Marina of the House of Saenz, equalled that of his father. God had blessed his parents with eight daughters and three sons, Ignatius being the youngest of the sons.

Right from the beginning, God had a plan for this child. Ignatius was sent to his aunt's castle where he received a solid Christian education and was prepared to enter King Ferdinand's service initially as a page. It is in the King's castle that Ignatius would lend his services to a young lady of the court as her knight. A gentleman, he never mentions her name in the poetry he writes at this time, but refers to her as *"more than a Countess or Duchess."* Some historians have conjectured that possibly the lady was the very young widow of King Ferdinand. Of course, marriage was out of the question, so our young knight loved from afar, serving in the noble way befitting his and her station. He wrote his most beautiful poetry at this time.

He was an avid reader, his taste leaning toward books on chivalry, knights and ladies of the court, recounting tales of glorious times of valor and honor. So, it is no surprise, we find him, in 1517, at twenty-six years of age, leaving to engage in his first battle, the defense of Navarre of which his uncle was Viceroy. The attack was suppressed by the Spaniards; but the French renewed their offensive and this time captured Navarre, and laid siege on Pamplona. Ignatius and the other Spanish soldiers were in the garrison, heavily outnumbered. Victory was impossible; but Ignatius was able to convince the others to remain with him and defend the fort.

The walls of the fortress began to crumble beneath the furious battery of cannon balls striking at its ramparts, quickly tearing down the soldiers' defenses and with that their hope of victory. Knowing the end was near and they would die, Ignatius turned to a good friend and asked him to hear his confession.[1] He fought courageously, right up to the moment a heavy cannon ball pierced the wall where Ignatius was fighting, shattered the bone of his right leg and seriously injured the other. When he fell, the others surrendered and the French soldiers captured the fort. But seeing how bravely he had fought, the French carried him to his rooms in town and had their physicians attend him for close to fifteen days. When they realized they were limited, the French had a litter made to carry the brave little soldier home. His small frame bobbing up and down on the litter (Ignatius was barely 5'2"), his red hair matted by the sweat pouring down his face from the intense pain, Ignatius never let out a cry!

It is not known why the bones did not set properly. Was it that he had been moved too soon or was it the arduous trip back home? Back at the Castle of Loyola, the doctors decided that the bones had to be broken again. Again, brave and noble knight, he asked for no form of anesthetic and went through the operation with his hands and teeth clenched. He grew weaker and weaker. The doctors advised him he was dying. Ignatius called for a priest and asked to receive the Last Rites of the Church. Ignatius would not last the night.

But again, God had another plan. The eve of the Feast of Sts. Peter and Paul, at midnight, Ignatius passed the crisis. Now, he had always had a devotion to St. Peter, and historians all agree that Ignatius had an apparition of St. Peter who told him he would be cured, and he was!

The physicians messed up the operation and a bone was left protruding from his leg. Ignatius had it removed. His friends marveled at the courage and strength shown by Ignatius

---

[1] "This confession, made to a layman in default of a priest, was an act of penance and humiliation, and shows that the warriors of those times did not consider it a weakness to think of their soul in the hour of danger." Life of St. Ignatius of Loyola by Fr. Genelli, S.J. - TAN Publications

throughout the operation, insisting they could not have endured the excruciating pain. The bones were straightened out at last, no bones protruding, but the operation left him with one leg shorter than the other.

His recovery was slow and arduous. Ignatius had an active mind, but it was locked up inside a body which was betraying him. But he could read! His mind and heart never left the young lady he had left behind. Now, he waited for the time when he would return and tell her how she had occupied his every thought in battle and as he was recuperating. He practiced over and over again what he would wear and what he would say. To prepare himself, he requested books on knighthood and ladies of the court. But (as God would plan it), in the Castle of Loyola there were only books on the life of Jesus and of the Saints!

Soon he found that contemplating things of the world gave him momentary pleasure, which soon faded away in the light of what he was reading about the graces from *Above!* Through the lives of Jesus and the Saints he was discovering a *new* world and a new *battlefield!* The Saints taught him he had to make a choice between the kingdom of Satan and the Kingdom of God. Their lives became strategic maps revealing the great battles needed to be waged, in order to gain eternal victory. All the vain glory he had sought in the past went up like so much smoke, when he discovered the sweet fragrance that was his to give, the offering he was being called to make to God the Creator. He discovered there was only one true, *lasting* glory in that which makes the *"soul pure and like unto God."*[2]

He spent long hours grieving for the sins of his past, coupled with his deep resolve to lead a life resembling that of the Desert Fathers and the Saints. The struggles and battles, fought between powers and principalities, for his soul at this time, run through the pages of Ignatius' book: *Spiritual Exercises.* Ignatius decided he would choose God and His ways; then God began to

---

[2] Life of St. Ignatius of Loyola by Fr. Genelli, S.J.

manifest Himself to him. One night, Ignatius was praying before the image of Our Lady, tears spilling from his eyes, pleading with God to show him He had accepted Ignatius, when a tremor shook the house, the walls began to crumble in his room; the window frames cracked. Ignatius rejoiced! He knew this was a sign - God was answering him and he would never be alone again; God was showing him that it was *He* Who was directing his life!

His Purgatory on earth coming to an end, Our Lady made an appearance and let him know how she had been interceding on his behalf. She was holding the Baby Jesus in Her arms; She said nothing; but Her presence filled his heart with a sweet peace unlike anything he had ever known. Before leaving, she bestowed another gift on him, one that would remain with him forever: He lost all desire for things and creatures of this world, as his soul was filled with the *"purity of the angels,"* and this gift would protect him, the rest of his life.

The Honeymoon begins between God and Ignatius

His days and nights were filled with grace upon grace from God; He was preparing Ignatius to share in His Passion, His rejection, His abandonment. Ignatius decided the only way he could know how to truly walk in Jesus' Footsteps was to go to the Holy Land, to where He walked, lived and died. He believed with all his heart that this was the only path he could take, to prepare himself for a life of penance and mortification, by which he might make up for his sins and those of the world. Then he would enter the Carthusian Monastery in Seville upon his return.

Now, although he did not share his conversion and the thoughts that were going through his mind and heart, all around him sensed a tremendous change coming about. He raised his thoughts more and more to the *eternal world*. He later wrote, having beheld Heaven, he would weep, crying out, *"Oh, how vile this earth seems when I look at Heaven."* This detachment from earth and its temptations, focusing on Heaven alone, would be the first of his *Spiritual Exercises*. It led him to understand that *"the end of man is not to serve the creature but God the Creator, and Him alone."*[3]

Ignatius defends his Lady against a Moor

Ignatius spoke to his older brother, of his desire to leave the castle, and all it represented, and begin a new life. His brother, believing that Ignatius would not *knowingly* do anything to bring dishonor on the family name, shared some of his concerns. Ignatius graciously listened and assured his brother he was aware of his duty; as a matter of fact, his first step would be to visit their relative, the Duke of Najera and apprise him of his plans. He stopped at his relative, shared briefly his new life with him, paid off a debt he had incurred, received a reluctant blessing and left for Montserrat.

Being too weak to walk, he mounted his mule and began his journey. He was meditating on the Blessed Mother when, who should he encounter but a *converso*.[4] The two began traveling together, when his companion asked Ignatius his destination. When he replied he was going to visit Our Lady of Montserrat, the man shared that although he believed Mary was a Virgin at the time of Jesus' Birth, she did not remain a Virgin. Ignatius insisted, he could not understand how, this man, as a Catholic, could choose to accept one truth and deny another. When his companion realized that he was trying to apostatize someone who knew his Faith and was not about to be dissuaded, he left Ignatius at the first fork in the road. Ignatius, the more incensed he became over what the follower of Mohammed had said, argued with himself if he should pursue the man and continue to try to convince him of his errors, or give him a good beating for so having maligned his Heavenly Mother. As this

---

[3]p.45 Life of St. Ignatius of Loyola by Fr. Genelli, S.J.
[4]These were either Moslems or Jews who had pretended to convert, but instead taught their own beliefs. Read more on this in Bob and Penny Lord's chapter on Saint Teresa of Avila in their book: *Saints and other Powerful Women in the Church.*

latter behavior would have suited the warrior and not the apostle he planned to become, Ignatius decided to continue his journey, with the idea of praying for this poor misguided man.

Now, Montserrat is an extremely high mountain; its ridges, like the teeth of a saw[5] made the climb perilous, at best. It not only looked impenetrable, it was that and more, its cliffs rising sharply with little or no plateaus. The only way to get to the top was by climbing treacherous steps cut out in the rock, by those who had dared to go before. Before beginning his ascent, Ignatius stopped at the church, at the foot of the mountain. There was a monk there, known for his holiness. Ignatius confessed his sins and shared all that he believed the Lord was calling him to do. For three days, he poured out his heart! This completed, the monk directed him, as an act of total abandonment to leave his mule at the monastery, and Ignatius obeyed. Then asking him if he was truly committed to depending solely on the Lord, he asked Ignatius if he could leave the only means of defense he would have from attacks leveled by any of God's creatures, two-legged as well as four-legged; would he leave his sword and dagger at the altar of Our Lady?

Our Lady's knight keeps guard over her during the night.

God, by His perfect Divine Design placed Ignatius at the foot of Montserrat on the Feast of the Annunciation. He decided he would stand guard over his Lady, *"keeping the night-watch of arms"*[6] as was the ancient practice of knights, before receiving their final war regalia. But instead of being attired in the resplendent coat of arms and regalia of a noble knight, he put aside his rich clothes and put on the robes of a poor penitent.[7] He donned a pilgrim's tattered robe of coarse fabric; removing his velvet and satin sash, he bound his waste with a rough cord; he replaced his boots of fine leather with hemp slip-ons. As his leg

[5]from which it got its name
[6]p.50 Life of St. Ignatius of Loyola by Fr. Genelli, S.J.
[7]which he had purchased on the way to Montserrat

had not healed entirely, he had to balance himself precariously on one foot, propping himself on a roughly whittled walking-stick.

With the rising of a new day, the knight of the House of Loyola was no more; this knight would fight the impossible fight, only for the Lord and His Mother. Staff in hand and a shell with which to scoop water to drink from a brook, all was in order. Now off to conquer the unseen foe! Onward to Montserrat! He began his ascent.

As God would have it, a future benefactor, Agnes Pasquale was to encounter Ignatius at Montserrat. As Montserrat was only nine miles from Manresa, where she was staying, it was not only her custom to go there, each Sunday, but as this was the Feast of the Assumption, to be there once again, to visit her Heavenly Mother. Mid-day, when she and her companions approached the Chapel of the Apostles, she could not help noticing a pilgrim who, although dressed as an indigent beggar, had an air of gentility about him. She was impressed by the piety which his eyes reflected the rare times he looked up; and his *humility* when they were cast down. Now, no longer able to walk, Ignatius inquired of the ladies if there was a hospital nearby. Agnes suggested he come with them to the one in Manresa. Refusing a ride on a donkey, Ignatius slowly followed the young women to Manresa. It was then that an officer of the law stopped him, inquiring if it were true that he had given his fine clothes to a destitute beggar; as they had not believed him, they had placed him in jail. Ignatius was truly grieved that he had caused the man this pain, and admitted that it was true; but would answer no further questions about himself.

Always seeking anonymity, preferring the company of God alone, he was much upset when word got out of what he had done. Life in Manresa was simple; Ignatius attended Mass daily, participated in Vespers, and received Holy Communion once a week. He would pray on his knees as much as seven hours a day. He rarely slept, scourged himself, begged for a small dry piece of bread, and drank a bit of water. His pilgrim's robe not penance enough, he wore a hair shirt next to his skin. He served the poor and the sick of the hospital, choosing those with the worst diseases. But although he kept the company of beggars, no one took him to be a beggar; consequently the children made fun of him; they chased him, calling him all sort of vile names. Only once, was he tempted to remove his humble attire, the abuse got so bad. Although he overcame that temptation, he felt it was time for him to seek more solitude, if he were to hear God speaking to him of His Will.

Ignatius discovers God in a cave

Ignatius discovered a dark cave, virtually unknown because it was so overgrown with brush. There, he would spend hours, sometimes all through the night, praying without interruption, except for the occasional sounds of God's four-legged and winged creatures calling out to one another. The cave at Manresa was a battlefield, a lonely battlefield, with Ignatius battling one temptation, winning that battle only to be put to the test with another temptation and another battle. Among other struggles, he imagined himself guilty of all types of sins, mistaking venial sin for mortal sin, battling alleged scruples and scrupulosity to the point of near desperation. He did not know where to turn; it seemed to him that God had deserted him. Then, he remembered hearing that God would come to his aid, if he fasted until his petition was granted. He fasted from Sunday to the following Sunday. His Spiritual Director seeing him dangerously weakened by this excessiveness, near death, ordered him to eat some food or he would deny him absolution. Ignatius obeyed and his melancholy left him!

Temptations of one kind or the other persisted until his trial over, his doubts and anxieties were also at an end. It had been one of the severest duels of his life; it seemed as if he were fencing with the prince of darkness himself, with the devil thrusting and him parrying, Ignatius, God's holy knight falling, appearing at times to be down for the last time, mortally wounded; but with the force of the Holy Spirit Who never left him, he would rise again to fight another battle. This time in the cave of Manresa would fill a spiritual well with teachings from which not only Jesuits would draw lifegiving water of knowledge and strength but those who in the future would read the Spiritual Exercises and follow Ignatius and his experiences to a deeper life with God.

He had fought! The lessons, received from both the powers of Heaven and hell would serve to form the vessel which God was shaping for His purpose. But it was not easy for Ignatius to follow what he called the *"Finger of God!"* He would say *"that God had treated him as a wise master does a child, to whom He gives little to learn at a time, and before whom He does not place a second lesson until he has well understood the first."*

Ignatius is visited by the forces of Heaven and hell!

Without the battles fought and won in the cave of Manresa, Ignatius could not have begun writing his *Spiritual Exercises*. Ignatius had visions of *the serpent* early in his spiritual life, before he had any Heavenly ecstasies.

Day had settled into night, wiping away the slightest ray of light entering his room at the hospital in Manresa, when Ignatius saw a figure, glowing and almost incandescent; it boldly intruded into his thoughts and prayers. Strain as he might, he could not recognize the figure; it was hard to identify, it was so blurred; all he could make out was that it dimly resembled a *serpent!* As he was almost hypnotized by the sight, suddenly blinding lights shot forth from what appeared to be many eyes on the form. Then it would leave. The image would return over and over again; Ignatius began to look forward to its next reappearance, feeling an unexplainable attraction toward it. But the Lord is always balancing the odds, always providing us with the ammunition to fight the attacks of the devil.

Ignatius would later in life write that while he was immersed in ecstasy, God infused him with such knowledge and enlightenment that if he were to add all he had received his entire life, it would not equal what he had learned in that one moment. When he came out of the ecstasy, he ran to the cross, in front of which he always prayed, and began to share his feelings with Jesus Crucified, when all of a sudden the glistening figure appeared! But this time, in the True Light of the Cross, Ignatius could perceive clearly who the vision was; it was the *father of deception* himself who had been appearing to Ignatius. This vision persisted, appearing again in Manresa and then in Rome, and then in Paris; but now Ignatius was able to quickly discern who it was and he dispelled him, at times attacking the vision with his bare hands and at other times disdainfully shooing him away with his walking stick.

Ignatius, because of the spiritual work God had planned for him to do, and the seeds of wisdom he would be called to sow, received the same infused knowledge from the Holy Spirit which other great Saints of his time, Spanish ones like Saints Teresa and John of the Cross had, of the Divine Mysteries of our Faith. One day, in the church of the Dominicans, while reciting the Little Office of the Blessed Virgin, he had a vision of the Holy Trinity. It had such a profound effect on him, he began to cry; from that day he entered into such intimacy with the Triune God that later in life this Divine Mystery would be the center of his prayer life and revelations. Another time, he was filled with the mystery of how God created the universe. Although he spoke of this, he, along with others who have seen Heaven, could not put into words what it was like being in the Kingdom and in the presence of those who dwelled therein. In this same church, when the Host was raised in consecration, he had a vision of the Child Jesus Who revealed how He was present in the Sacred Host after the consecration.

He had interior visions of the God-Man Jesus, seeing Him with the eyes of his heart, between 20-40 times. He had visions of the Blessed Mother as well, in the same way. When hospitalized in the Hospital of St. Lucy, he went into ecstasy for a whole week, beginning with Saturday lasting until the following

Saturday. He lay as if dead, with the faintest heartbeat. When he came to, as if awakening from a deep sleep, he cried out over and over again, *"O Jesus! Jesus!"* This was reported by eye-witnesses who had been at his bedside. Ignatius never spoke of what had transpired during that ecstasy. There are those who ascertain that it was then that he received the word to establish the *"Company of Jesus,"* for when he was writing the Constitution of the Jesuits, he would say that he was including certain passages that were given to him at Manresa. The Jesuits say one thing is definite, Ignatius was given the idea of the Company of Jesus while meditating on the Kingdom of Jesus Christ.

Before leaving Manresa, Ignatius would have more serious bouts with his health, each time almost succumbing to the *angel of death*; but God was not finished using him. Ignatius, this selfless, caring vessel of God so touched young men, they flocked to him. But for as many as loved him and hung on his every word, there were those who hated him and the change that was coming about among the people; and so they began maligning not only Ignatius but all those holy families who were befriending him. He had no recourse but to leave Manresa. His ten month stay at Manresa over, he left with only the patched clothes of a pauper on his back; but he was accompanied by the love and prayers of all whom he had touched. As he did not speak Latin, they begged him to take a companion who could assist him in Italy. He refused saying, all he needed was faith, hope and charity:

"If he took a companion, he would be looking to him for food when hungry, and if he fell would look to him to lift him up, and would thus be learning to rest in him, whereas he desired only to love and look up to God, and put all his hope and confidence in Him. `And the pilgrim,' said St. Ignatius of himself, `spoke from his heart.'"[8]

---

[8]St. Ignatius always speaks in the third person, humbly calling himself the

Ignatius leaves for Barcelona, his sites on the Holy Land

His heart saddened at leaving so many dear ones, his soul soared at the prospect of being one step closer to the Holy Land and his dream to convert the unbelievers. Ignatius arrived in Barcelona, and there met Doña Isabel Roser, who saw him encircled in light while he was praying. She helped him gain free passage to Italy on a ship, with the condition he would furnish his own provisions for the trip. Ignatius begged, and for the most part was given alms, but as always there are those who abuse the down-and-out. Afraid they would deny him if he said he was ultimately going to the Holy Land, considering the trip too dangerous, he begged just enough alms to get him to Rome, his first stop. One person, hearing he was going to Rome, answered *"Those who go to Rome, seldom come back the better for their visit."*[9]

Ignatius landed in Naples five days later, and traveled by foot with three other people, who like himself were begging for alms for their journey to Rome. One was a young man, and the other two a mother and daughter (disguised as a young man to protect her from being attacked). They were given food and a place to stay by some villagers, the mother and daughter a room on the top floor and Ignatius and the young man a place to sleep in the barn. At midnight, Ignatius became alarmed at the crying and screams coming from the rooms above. Hearing Ignatius shouting as he bolted up the stairs to defend the women, the attacker fled. Ignatius believed it must have been the young man, as he was not to be found when they set out for Rome.

Fearing they were carrying the plague, the little band of three were refused admission when they arrived at the gates of Rome. Especially Ignatius looked suspect, but when he explained he was not ill, but exhausted from his long trip, he was allowed to enter Rome. It was Palm Sunday, when Ignatius

---

"Pilgrim." Life of St. Ignatius of Loyola by Fr. Genelli, S.J.
[9]The same kind of tour guide who gave Luther false information.

arrived; he spent Holy Week visiting churches and making the Stations of the Cross, and that completed, left for Venice with a passport to the Holy Land, after having received the Pope's blessing. His poor clothes and equally poor health caused him much pain and problems as he traveled throughout Italy. Judging he had the plague, they would not allow him to enter *Venice* without a certificate affirming he had a clean bill of health. Alone, too tired to go on, he spent the night out in the cold. But although his human companions left him stranded, his Lord had not; God told Ignatius He would be with him and protect him. The next day, the guards at the gates of Venice did not notice Ignatius and he entered without the required papers.

Although too ill to make the voyage, Ignatius boarded the ship, and after having the customary sea-sickness was relieved of his raging fever. The sailors used the language of the gutter, never once considering the pilgrims aboard, especially women. When Ignatius scolded, they began to plot against him; they planned to leave him on a deserted island. But when they approached the island a furious wind whipped the ship toward the Isle of Cyprus, where other pilgrims were waiting. They walked thirty miles to the ship which would carry them to the Holy Land.

Ignatius arrived and rushed to tell the Franciscans (who were the custodians of the Holy Land), that his purpose in coming to the Holy Land was to park himself near the Holy Sepulcher of Our Lord and labor there to spread the Kingdom of Christ. He shared his plan to found a *Company of Jesus* committed to bringing the Word of God to the followers of Mohammed. The Franciscans agreed he could go about evangelizing, as long as he could provide for himself; but to await their Provincial for the final word. Ignatius went about his way, alone and with the other pilgrims, visiting all the holy places where his Savior had walked, right up to His last Walk to the Cross. The day before the other pilgrims were to depart, Ignatius was called before the Provincial, who ordered him to leave tomorrow with the other pilgrims. Ignatius was confused! The Provincial accused him of endangering himself and the other pilgrims. He said that if the Moslems had caught them they would have killed them or held them for ransom, and that Ignatius, remaining in the Holy Land, would not only be a threat to himself but to all the Franciscans.

The Provincial stated he had a Bull from the Pope declaring he had full authority, and to disobey him was to be excommunicated. Ignatius, believing this was the Will of the Lord, told the provincial it was not necessary to show him the Bull, he would obey! Ignatius departed for Venice. God was with him all the way! The ships which denied him passage were ship-wrecked and the poor ship he was on landed safely in Venice.

Ignatius takes the long road back to Spain

Ignatius traveled from Venice to Genoa; and war raging, first was taken prisoner by the Spanish as a spy for the French, and convincing them he was not, by the French as a spy for the Spanish. In Genoa he met a friend who gave him passage on his ship, and Ignatius reached Barcelona the early part of 1524. He rushed to Manresa to begin studying with a Cistercian monk he had known, but upon finding he had died, Ignatius returned to Barcelona. He was admitted into a public school where he would study Latin. His old friend Doña Isabel Roser and others helped him, providing him a place to stay and food. The servants learning he was of the nobility treated him cruelly, accusing him of being a bum who ran away from his duties. He prayed for them, and they were converted before he left. To further his walk to the Cross, here he was thirty-three years old struggling to learn among much younger, brilliant students who breezed through their Latin lessons.

John Pasquale, son of one of his benefactors, said that he would look in on Ignatius and would see him, deep in prayer, his knees bent, levitated, exclaiming *"O Lord, if men only knew Thee!"* To his embarassment, this would also happen in public.

At a convent, after having prayed for over three hours, he was seen rising, levitating for a long time.

Ignatius never compromised his mission and commitment to God. There was a convent of Nuns who had gone so far from their vow of closure, they even had men visiting them in the parlor. Ignatius heard of this and began visiting the convent, praying hours on end for the conversion of the Nuns. Noting the piety of Ignatius, they asked him to speak to them. He spoke to them of their vocation, the vows they had taken, shared his Spiritual Exercises and before you know it, conversion came about. But not everyone was converted; there were those who liked the freedom they had; and in an effort to discourage him from returning, had him beaten several times on the road. That failing to deter him, they hired two Moorish slaves to kill him. They were waiting for him at the gate of the convent and beat him and his priest companion, so brutally, the priest died a few days later and Ignatius was close to death. As soon as he recovered, he went to the convent, over the pleading of his many friends who knew what had transpired. One of the men who had beaten him, begged his forgiveness and was converted.

Returning home from the convent, he came upon a man who had hanged himself. Ignatius drew near to the body which had been cut down from the tree. Not being able to revive him, Ignatius began praying and crying, begging God to have mercy on one who had died such a horrible death, condemning himself to eternal damnation. The man opened his eyes and expressed sorrow for all his sins, and having done so closed his eyes for the last time.

Ignatius was tested and consequently informed he was ready to study at the illustrious University of Alcala. Young men began to join his company; he had four by this time; like him they all lived on alms, wore the same long grey habit and a cap of matching color, gaining the name, the *ensacados* or men in sacks. Life for Ignatius was not only an *interior* walk, but one very much involved with the spiritual and physical well-being of his brothers and sisters, the poor of all kinds.

At the University, Ignatius saw a canon who, upon making the acquaintance of wild young men, began living a life unworthy of his vow. Ignatius prayed and then went to the home of the canon, who reluctantly let him in. After hours of Ignatius praying and reminding him of the gift he had been given by God, and the price Jesus paid for the salvation of his soul and those he was ordained to save, the canon's disdain and anger turned to deep respect and he was converted and resumed living up to his vocation.

Ignatius is called before the Inquisition!

Like with Jesus, although Ignatius desired to remain anonymous, helping others unnoticed and unrewarded, he came to the attention of the authorities and was brought before the Inquisition, for the first time. At the time of Ignatius and those other Spanish mystics Teresa and John of the Cross, there were many false prophets and alleged mystics flying around. There was a group of extremists who called themselves the *"Illuminati"* or enlightened ones. These *Alumbrados* were pseudo-mystic Spaniards who claimed to act always under illumination received directly and immediately from the Holy Spirit, and independently of the means of grace dispensed by the Church. These *Alumbrados* had infiltrated parts of Spain and were brought before the Tribunal of Toledo. Happenings like these, coupled with very few spiritual directors understanding the mystics of that day's spirituality made them suspect, and they all were called before the Tribunals or the Inquisition.

Ignatius' friends and acquaintances were questioned; the judge found nothing irregular in Ignatius behavior and turned him over to a Doctor of Theology who, after examining Ignatius and his companions, found no blame in them of faith or morals, and advised them they could continue their spiritual practices. The only proviso was that since they were not a recognized Religious Order, they alter their habits, if not in design in color. Ignatius and his little band of four obeyed!

The following year, another charge was leveled against Ignatius. The police came to his room and arrested him, never telling him the crime he was accused of. It turned out, the problem was that two women, a mother and daughter, under his spiritual direction, had wandered far afield from the limits he had placed on them and began to dress as paupers, going from one hospital to another, caring for the poor and sick. When they told Ignatius of their practice he cautioned them, pointing out the danger they opened themselves up to, as well as possible scandal; he ordered them to cease immediately and they obeyed. But toward the end of Lent they thought it would do no harm if they went on pilgrimage, begging alms on the way to various shrines. They brought one maid and told only a few close friends. But when their absence drew attention, and their friends were questioned, they had to reveal what the ladies were doing. As the two were from nobility and had an illustrious guardian, rather than allow this be a blemish on his and their reputation, poor Ignatius was blamed and imprisoned!

His incarceration did allow visitors, so many hearing of the *good samaritan's* fate, came and left saying things like, *"I have seen Paul in chains."* Forty-two days passed, and at last Ignatius was questioned. They found nothing against him and he was free to leave, under the condition (now he is innocent, right?) that he and his companions remove their habits and dress as the other students, and that he do no teaching in public or private before having completed his four years of philosophy. Should he disobey, he would be excommunicated! Ignatius agreed. But it was not that easy; so many had been enriched by his wisdom and teachings, for him to adopt the life of an ordinary student in Alcala, was impossible, and so Ignatius left for the University of Salamanca to resume his studies.

Ignatius arrived in Salamanca and since this was a different diocese and the restriction placed on him in the diocese of Alcala did not apply, Ignatius began giving spiritual help to those who came to him. It came to the attention of the

Dominicans who invited him to their convent and drilled him about things of the Faith, he answered brilliantly. The Vicar asked him how, with such a limited education in Theology, he was able to preach on vice and sin; and then trying to trap him (as the temple priests attempted with Jesus) he continued that since he had not been schooled in such matters of faith, he had to have been instructed by the Holy Spirit. Ignatius, after answering a battery of questions was placed, along with one of his company, in prison, *again*. Although he was again found innocent of any wrong-doing, Ignatius and his company were ordered to cease teaching the difference between venial and mortal sin, until their education was completed.

As Ignatius believed and rightly so, if you cannot preach about sin, you cannot call men to conversion; so although many begged him to stay, Ignatius knew he had to leave for the University of Paris. He arrived in Paris, but because of a lack of funds he had to go to begging once again, to some Spanish merchants. That accomplished he studied rhetoric for a year and a half, philosophy for three and a half years at which time he received the degree Doctor of Philosophy, and Theology for a year and a half, but he would not complete his studies in the University of Paris, because once again Ignatius would come under attack and have to eventually leave for Venice! It was 1535 and Ignatius was forty four years old.

However, while he was still in Paris, Ignatius sought and found men for his company. Three young men of prestigious backgrounds and advanced education renounced the world, consecrating themselves to this new life of poverty for the Lord. They sold all they had and gave it to the poor, beginning a life dependent on alms. Now, when this became known to their friends and a professor in particular, they *formally* accused Ignatius of witchcraft, and once again *Ignatius is brought before the Inquisition*. Now, couple this with the documents they retrieved from the various Tribunals held in Spain and we can see Ignatius is in trouble!

While this was all happening, a young man lodging with Ignatius, took what little alms Ignatius had to maintain himself and spent it frivolously. Then he left for Spain; but on the way became so ill he had to stop in Rouen. He wrote to Ignatius begging for help. Now, Ignatius was weakened by all the attacks he had sustained; his health was very poor; the idea of making this journey was abhorrent to him, but then he went into the church of the Dominicans and prayed.

The next day, before the sun rose, although he could barely stand, Ignatius was on his way to help the errant young man. It took him three days! Arriving in Rouen, he tended the young man, and no sooner had he recovered, a messenger brought Ignatius a letter from Paris advising him he had been brought before the Inquisition! Ignatius immediately went to a Notary with the messenger to obtain a document certifying that he had just received the word and had responded immediately; in this way to show that he had not gone to Rouen to escape appearing at the Inquisition.

Arriving in Paris, he immediately appeared before the Inquisitor! The Inquisitor found nothing against Ignatius and dismissed him, assuring him he had nothing to fear. But the damage was done; the three students who had joined him, left him. But other students resumed coming to Ignatius, and soon there were more at his conferences than at the professors' sessions; they were up in arms. One in particular went to Govéa, Rector of the university. Instead of sending a warning to Ignatius, if he did not cease his conferences, he would be subject to the *"aula,"*[10] they sent word to Ignatius to present himself in the public hall where he would be chastised and condemned by the masters in front of the whole student body. At first, Ignatius was happy to submit to this unjustified treatment, believing he would be sharing in his Lord's humiliation; but after praying he

---

[10]being chastised and berated, sometimes whipped, as punishment for being disobedient or some other act deserving discipline

realized that this would bring scandal, not so much on him, but on the *Spiritual Exercises* which were being used to feed the students spiritually.

Ignatius insisted he be brought before the Rector, before being punished. When Govéa heard Ignatius speak, he was so moved by his reasoning, he took him by the hand, walked him into the center of the hall and crying, begged his forgiveness. Now not only students, but professors came to Ignatius to learn about the Spiritual life.

Ignatius and his followers take their vows at Montmartre

Six students in the School of Divinity would join Ignatius; they were: Peter Faber, Francis Xavier, Laynez, Salmarom, Simon Rodriguez, and Nicholas Bobadilla.

Peter Faber was a brilliant student preparing for his ordination as a priest; he tried to work out all his temptations and doubts by himself, even hiding them from his Spiritual Director. Now, as God would have it, Peter and Ignatius shared the same room. Peter tried everything, fasting, harsh penances; finally one day with tears flowing down his flushed cheeks, he revealed the state of his soul. Suddenly he felt a wave of relief flow over him. Ignatius then began walking him through the Spiritual Exercises one day at at time, as the Lord had advised him, *"not teaching him the second, until the first was understood."* Peter Faber was ordained and became one of Ignatius' first disciples.

Ignatius went to lodge at St. Barbara's College where he would meet the young reluctant disciple *Francis Xavier.* Like Ignatius, Francis Xavier came from nobility, an old and illustrious family from the Basque country. He was a professor, specializing in Aristotle and philosophy. Whereas he had different plans, filled as he was with aspirations of the world, and rightfully judging they had nothing to do with Ignatius, he would find himself giving into God and His Will for him, and become known as co-founder of the Company of Jesus. He would go where Ignatius dreamed to go, but couldn't, to India and convert the unbelievers.

Others flocked to join Ignatius; but not everyone loved him! This one night, knowing he would be alone, a friend of Francis Xavier who hated Ignatius for the change that had come about in his friend and others, decided to steal into his room and assassinate him. A *voice* which remonstrated him, not only froze him to the spot and he did not complete his horrible sin, but he threw himself at Ignatius' feet and begged his forgiveness. Later, this same man will accuse Ignatius before an Inquisition.

The little Company of Jesus gathered and agreed to leave the matter up to the Lord: *If they could not go to Palestine nor preach where they were, they should venture to other countries and preach there. The plan was they should go to Jerusalem and place the problem before God. If there, the majority should decide to stay in the Holy Land, then the others would obey, taking it as the Will of God. But should the opposite be true, they would place themselves at the service of the Pope.* They decided to leave for Venice the 25th of January, 1537, after all their classes were completed, and chose the Feast of the Assumption of the Blessed Virgin to take their vows in a little Church of Our Lady of Montmartre. Father Peter Faber, who was the only priest in their company, celebrated the Mass.

Ignatius is ordained

Ignatius went by foot to his parent's home in Aspeitia; although they desired to give him a royal welcome, sensitive to his new life, they chose a humble one befitting his calling. He remained there three months during which time many miraculous healings came about. He went to the neighboring villages and settled the estates of his followers. And then all matters resolved, it was time for him to leave his friends and family; he struggled with the love he felt for them, as they tearfully begged him to remain. He traveled by sea back to Italy.

Weathering a treacherous voyage, he finally arrived in Genoa; and braving the icy cold winter, he walked across the Alps to Venice. There he was met by others of his company who had to leave Paris because a war had broken out. Always focusing on the positive, and on his mission, he and his companions planned to go to the Pope to get his permission to go to the Holy Land and receive *"Holy Orders under the title of voluntary poverty."*[11] As it was winter, they would not be able to set out for Rome till Lent began. Ignatius chose to remain behind, as there were men in Rome, opposed to him in the past, who might be prejudiced against their cause because of him. But one of these men, having laid aside his former bias, highly praised Ignatius and the work of his Company. Pope Paul III invited Ignatius' followers to partake in discussions on the tenets of the Faith, with some of his eminent theologians. He listened attentively and then said, *"I am truly so happy to find so much learning joined to so much humility; if I can assist you in anything, I will do so willingly."* The brothers had represented their founder well! The Pope gave his permission but added he doubted they would go, a war was about to break out.

Nevertheless the Pope gave Father Faber and his twelve companions permission, along with money to pay for their journey (which they repaid when as the Pope predicted, the journey became impossible). On the 24th of June, 1537 Ignatius, now 45 years old, and those of his company who had as not yet received Holy Orders were ordained priests forever according to the Order of Melchisedech. Ignatius, hoping to celebrate his first Mass on Calvary, waited a year and a half before celebrating his first Mass at the Chapel of the Holy Crib[12] in the Church of St. Mary Major in Rome, sighing it was the closest he could come to Bethlehem.

The little band broke up into small groups and went preaching into the neighboring towns of northern Italy. Ignatius and his company were given a dilapidated, deserted convent without windows or any furnishings, where they slept on the floor. Ignatius began speaking of God, and the faithful always

[11]p.172 Life of St. Ignatius of Loyola by Fr. Genelli, S.J.
[12]tradition tells us this is the Crib where Jesus was born.

hungering for the Divine, the numbers grew and so did the avarice and jealousy! So once more Ignatius is called before the Inquisition. The Vicar General Legate in Venice came against him. Although the accusations had already been discredited by the findings of the Inquisition in Paris, Ignatius insisted on having a certificate drawn which would formally affirm his innocence. He got his wish, was again exonerated, and his doctrine declared irreproachable! They met in Vicenza and Ignatius gave them the name of the *Society of Jesus*; he told them that taking Jesus as their Chief and Model they were to go out and bring the Good News to all the world.

Father Ignatius, Father Faber and Father Laynez went to Rome, where Ignatius had a vision at La Storta, a village six miles from Rome. Ignatius shared with Father Faber that "God had imprinted on his mind, *'I will be favorable to you in Rome.'"*[13] He said that he did not know what God meant; he thought maybe it was that they were to be crucified there. Then he said that Jesus appeared to him carrying the Cross and beside Him was God the Father Who said to Our Lord, *"I will that Thou take this man for Thy servant."* Then Ignatius said that Jesus took him and said, *"I will that thou serve Me."*[14]

Once again Ignatius is accused of heresy, found innocent and after appealing to Pope Paul III is officially exonerated! Famine devastates Rome, and Ignatius and his followers pick up the dying and the starving people of Rome from out of the gutters, bring them into their modest convent and share what little they have to eat. The rich, seeing how these men feed the poor in body and spirit, bringing them the love of Jesus, were moved to pity and began generously contributing to the cause. Through this, many charitable institutions were begun in Rome which till today care for orphans and all those who cannot care for themselves.

---

[13]Life of St. Ignatius of Loyola by Fr. Genelli, S.J.
[14]Life of St. Ignatius of Loyola by Fr. Genelli, S.J.

The Company of Jesus takes their solemn vows

The first draft of their Constitution was approved and it was time for the little company to elect a superior. Ignatius called all the members in Italy, to come together for this holy purpose, during the holiest times of the year, Lent. Those who were far away in foreign lands, sent their votes back in sealed envelopes. The only one who abstained from voting was Ignatius, who did not want to show favor for one above the others. He said he would abide by their decision. Little did he realize he would want to eat those words. To his deep consternation he was unanimously elected as superior (of course with one abstention, his own)! He had never wished to be looked up to, as founder; he was just one of the Company of Jesus; Jesus was the Founder, the Lord of all.

He begged; he pleaded, to no avail! They were adamant! When he implored them to vote again, taking in consideration his desire to be just one of them, with one of the other brothers taking the reins, they did; and the results were the same! Ignatius turned to his confessor for help; he appealed to him to explain why he could not accept the position of leadership, that he felt himself totally unworthy and unqualified for such a responsibility. After much prayer, his confessor returned to Ignatius with a sealed envelope containing the results of his prayerful meditations.

The envelope was opened and read before the entire assembly: *Ignatius must submit to the wishes of his community and accept the responsibility of superior.* The cheering finally subsiding, it was time for them to gather together and take their solemn vows at the church of St. Paul outside the walls. They made the Stations of the Cross in other churches in Rome and then celebrated the Sacrifice of the Mass in Our Lady's chapel in St. Paul's Basilica, which was also the Chapel of the Blessed Sacrament.

At that moment when it was time for Ignatius to give Holy Communion to his brothers, he raised the Host above the paten and intoned aloud their vows. Then he repeated this for each of his brothers before they received their Beloved Lord in the Eucharist. With this act of love and adoration, they were pledging their lives to their Lord Present among them. It was to Him they were making their vows, and it was fitting it be in this chapel where He reigned, for all to come and adore, and where His Most Precious Mother was also present. All having joined in this holy endeavor, the Army of Jesus was ready to serve and die for their Church and her Vicar if need be. When the Mass was over, all of the Company came onto the Altar, embraced Ignatius and one another, tears unashamedly spilling from their eyes. The vow they took is the following:

"I, the undersigned, promise to God Almighty, and to the Pope, His Vicar upon earth, in the presence of the Blessed Virgin, His Mother, and in the presence of the Society, perpetual poverty, chastity, and obedience, according to the form contained in the Bull of the Society of Our Lord Jesus Christ, and in the Constitutions already published, or which shall be published afterwards. I promise, moreover, particular obedience to the Pope with regard to the mission spoken of in the Bull. I promise likewise to take care that the youth be instructed in the doctrines of the Faith according to the same Bull and the Constitutions. Given at Rome, Friday, the 22nd of April, in the Church of St. Paul beyond the walls."
Ignatius of Loyola

Ignatius opens a house for penitents and former prostitutes.

Ignatius is again falsely accused and brought before the Tribunal. Ignatius opened St. Martha, a house for penitents and former prostitutes. Now there was a man who had corrupted the wife of another and was living in sin, with her in Rome. Through Ignatius, she repented and entered the House of St. Martha. Matthias, the man in question was furious and brought charges against Ignatius. He was a man of influence and he soon turned many of Ignatius' benefactors against him. Ignatius insisted the matter be investigated. The Pope's Vicar came to the house of

St. Martha and again Ignatius' teachings were investigated and all found in order. The woman in question and her husband, being of the nobility, asked Ignatius to quietly accept Matthias' apology, and let the matter rest. But Ignatius insisted the Tribunal judge the matter. And again, all allegations against Ignatius were found false; Matthias was chastised by the court and made to absorb the costs of the Tribunal. Then, even he was converted and became one of the Society of Jesus' benefactors.

Ignatius founded a house for catechumens or Jewish converts. Now, because the authorities had taken advice from Ignatius, the priest in charge of the house, in a rage of jealousy filed false charges against Ignatius, accusing him of heresy and breaking the seal of confession. He insisted on the matter being scrupulously investigated. What resulted was that the priest was investigated and found guilty of wrongdoing, which he had been able to hide, and by his own confession, calumny. He lost his faculties and all his benefices, as well as his place and goods were confiscated. The court condemned him to life imprisonment, which through the intercession of Ignatius was reduced to exile.

Ignatius prepares to go Home, at last Sweet Jesus, Home!

Early in 1555, Ignatius began showing signs of going Home! Although most of his life he was on the edge, holding onto life with his fingernails, as if saying to the Lord, *Not now, I have too much to do!* Now, this was different; there was nothing left; he had no more to give, but give he would till he closed his eyes for the last time. In 1556, his days now numbered, he wrote to his dear friend and benefactor, Doña Elenora Mascarena. Answering her request he pray for Prince Philip, whom she had nursed as a baby, he wrote that he had prayed for him when he was a young prince, but since ascending to the throne, he prayed for him twice as much. And now that he was dying Ignatius said he would pray for him and for her in Heaven.

As if leaving his last will and testament, he said,

"I have desired above all others three things, and thanks

to God, I see them all accomplished-that the Company should be confirmed by the Pope, that the book of the Spiritual exercises should be approved by the Holy See, and thirdly that the Constitutions should be completed and observed in the whole Society. "[15]

Ignatius predicted his death

Thursday, the day before he died, he asked Father Polanco to send a message to his Holiness that he was dying, and to ask him for a blessing for himself and for Father Olave who was also dying.[16] He said to tell his Holiness that if he had the grace to go to Heaven, he would pray for him, as he did on earth while alive. Thinking he was not seriously ill as he talked with them and ate a good meal that evening, Father Polanco thought it best to wait till Friday to notify the Holy See. The next morning, it was obvious the holy knight Ignatius was dying. His agony lasted a short time; the Pope was notified and with much grief gave him the Apostolic Blessing for his last voyage *Home.* Ignatius went peacefully to his Beloved Mother Mary and Her Son Jesus. It was the last day of July, 1556.

Ignatius, priest, founder and knight was canonized in 1622.

Sleep well, loyal and holy knight of the Papacy.

Sadly, there is not enough room to go into all his struggles, being accepted and then rejected, being accused and then exonerated to be accused again. But through it all, he remained a loyal son of the Church! Born at the same time as one of the deadliest movements to attack Mother Church, God raised up a giant! He truly was a servant of Jesus. I know of no one in the history of the Church who had more reason to give up, but Ignatius persisted; a soldier he fought the impossible fight and his sons have had this heritage to challenge them and fortify them. Writing about Ignatius of Loyola has brought us to deeper

---

[15]Life of St. Ignatius of Loyola by Fr. Genelli, S.J
[16]At the time Father Olave was not even sick. He became ill on August 6th and died shortly after.

understanding of our brothers, the Society of Jesus. Family of Jesus, we have fallen in love with your founder. There is a popular saying, *What would Jesus do?*   Now, when making decisions, ask yourselves, *What would Ignatius do?*

Above: *Convent of the Incarnation, Avila, Spain*

Above: *St. Teresa of Avila Doctor of the Church Reformer of the Carmelites*
Below: *Avila - Birthplace of St. Teresa*

Above: *St. Teresa of Avila with St. John of the Cross*

Below: *Death of St. Teresa in Alba de Tormes, Spain*

Left: *Statue of St. Teresa of Avila in the Shrine of her Birthplace, Avila, Spain*

Saint Teresa of Avila
True Reformer of the Church

In times of crisis, when it looks as if hell will prevail against His Church, God sends down powerful men and women to defend her. Teresa was one of those women!

When I look about me at the grave times we live in, and want to *run* or at best *live* on an island, I think of *Santa Teresa la Grande!* She was born into the worst of times, times very much like today. But like other Saints of the Counter-Reformation, like God Who turned the *sorrowful* Passion into a *glorious* Resurrection, she would turn the dire times of the Sixteenth Century into a time of *true* Reform.

Is this not what our Pope John Paul II is trying to do, today? Is he not counteracting the heretics from within our Church, who are threatening to sink the Ship of the Church by bringing about a Grand Renewal? Do we not have a Teresa of Avila in our midst - Mother Angelica - who *fears not the terror of the night, nor the arrow that flies by day?*[1] Will she not go down in the annals of our Church, as one of the key Counter-Reformers of our day?

And how are they counter-reforming the Church? By teaching the *truth*, as it has been passed down through the centuries; by taking action to expose heresies and heretics; by correcting the errors disseminated, with the true teaching of the Magisterium; finally checking the harm done and ultimately purging the Church of the venom that has been slowly poisoning her.

This was what Teresa and all those who bear the title, Defender of the Church did; and so long as the enemy persists in his action to prevail against the Church, the fair *Bride of Christ*, God will raise Counter-Reformation Saints to battle and claim victory for the Roman Catholic Church!

Teresa lived through some of the most tragic days of the

---

[1]Ps91:5,6

Church, with brother fighting brother, the cruelest blows coming from within; the trusted sons of Mary, dissident bishops and priests like Luther, instigating warfare against Her Son's Church. The attack came from those closest to Mother Church,[2] and since the greatest pain is when you are attacked by a loved one, one of the family, the Church was wounded and vulnerable. Not wanting to lose a son, but ever prudent Mother Church had no recourse but to warn the erring child, censure him, and then when he refused to obey, ex-communicate him. When Luther placed himself above the Church, I am sure he could not see the far-reaching ramifications of his actions. But the harm that man does, does not stay confined to him alone, but scatters in the breeze like so many down feathers, blowing where they may, landing as far as the winds will take them.

Europe was being taken over, inch by inch, mile by mile, by an advancing army; only it was deadlier than most *worldly* armies, in that it used the Holy Name of Jesus. Calvinism and Lutheranism, spread throughout much of Europe but was not going to take over Spain! Teresa came into the world from a country which, having suffered over 700 years without Jesus and His Church, would not cave in under the subterfuge and pressure from protesters[3] calling rebellion "*Reformation.*" Spain would raise up Defenders of the Faith, like Teresa of Avila, Ignatius of Loyola, John of the Cross and a host of others who would defend Mother Church, even when they were being attacked, suffering condemnation and calumny,[4] from those within the Church. But they did not stop! This is why they were born; this was their mission-to fight the foe, no matter the cost.

Teresa said her primary reason for being, was to combat and counteract the ills brought about by Luther's disobedience. She wrote: "*It seems to me that I could fight all alone against all*

---

[2]This was not unusual, as from the very beginning most of the heresies attacking the very foundation of our Church came from within.
[3]Protestants
[4]slander

the Lutherans to make them understand their error. I feel deeply the loss of so many souls."

To answer those who would defend Luther, at the cost of maligning the Church, insisting he had good intentions and wanted to correct a fault within the Church, we go to Saint Teresa's words, *"to accomplish a good, however great it may be, even a small evil is not to be done."* This was her philosophy, a lesson she learned while still quite young. But then this is not about Luther but about Teresa who brought about change, always *a faithful daughter of the Church.*[5]

Teresa would be just one of the victims of the Reformation (or more aptly Rebellion), but although her suffering was at times staggering, she obeyed; she did not rebel; she brought about change through faith in God, always holding onto Jesus' words to her. When she felt totally empty and alone, with no friends to console her, Jesus came and stood beside her, *"Have no fear, daughter, for I am here, and I will not forsake you, have no fear."*

Obedience, faith and waiting upon God's timetable was her vanguard. But do not think Teresa just sat back and did nothing; her whole life was one of prayer, penance and action! *"Teresa, always calling herself a sinner, was to do penance throughout her life in reparation for what she considered `this evil brought about by Luther.'"*

[A former Jewess, Saint Edith Stein,[6] who converted to the Roman Catholic Church, after having read Teresa's autobiography, spoke with the same heart and mind as Teresa her mentor, as she was being led to the gas chambers in Auschwitz[7] to die, ***"If I do not pray and do retribution for the Germans, who will?"*** *"...she was dying as a Jewess and Catholic Nun for the Jews who were being persecuted because they believed in*

---

[5]paraphrasing Teresa's last words
[6]canonized October 11, 1998 by the same Pope who beatified her on May 1st, 1987, Pope John Paul II
[7]Nazi concentration camps in Poland

the One God, and as a German for the Germans who were persecuting the Jewish people."[8]

The Church comes under a new attack!

The fight to restore Christianity did not end with the expulsion of the Moors. Not even the thick walls of Avila,[9] forty feet high and thirteen feet thick, could keep out the conflict and confusion. What began in the Thirteenth Century, carried over to the Fourteenth and Fifteenth Centuries, growing into a struggle between neighbors - between Christians and Jews, as well as *Conversos* who were Jews who had converted to Christianity in name only; some of them out of fear and others out of expediency. Now, there are never all *bad* guys and all *good* guys; man with his inborn weakness to sin often gives into the temptations of the devil and goes astray. Part of the problem facing the Church and the State was that some of the *Conversos* were Priests, Bishops, and Cardinals who were teaching heresy to the unsuspecting faithful!

The Spanish Inquisition

False prophets, false teaching, mass confusion and illusory[10] apostasy, would all lead to the Inquisition, which would ultimately affect Teresa. The Spanish Inquisition! We Catholics have hung our heads in shame for many years, most of us not knowing what the Inquisition *was*, no less *about*, with our separated brothers and sisters in Christ, no more knowledgeable than we (Catholics) repeating old lies, unaware of their origin or veracity.

Let us begin by trying to explain the Spanish Inquisition, which was instituted by King Ferdinand and Queen Isabella, by special authorization of the Holy See in 1476. Its purpose was primarily to *protect* conversos and Jewish converts, from the

[8]from Bob and Penny Lord's chapter on Edith Stein in their book: *"Martyrs, They died for Christ"*
[9]raised between 1090 and 1097
[10]deceptive

retaliation of their fellow men and from relapse; then to seek out lapsed Jewish converts with the idea of *teaching* them more on the Faith, so that they would not fall into error; and finally to *prevent* the relapse of Moorish converts, and keep them from forming harmful alliances with various heretical groups. Sadly, whenever man gets involved, good turns into bad, what was meant to heal hurts; the Inquisition became *a tool of the state*, which eventually persecuted and abused the Jewish people, but not in the exaggerated numbers historically reported.

When you start to judge Spain and her Catholic Regents, King Ferdinand and Queen Isabella, you must remember that Spain had been just reconquered, after over seven hundred years of domination and enslavement by the Moors, where belief in Jesus was a death sentence. With the recovery of Spain for Christ and His Church, the people of Spain were at last seeing some light. But they were vulnerable. Not having had the Faith taught for so many centuries, they were open to error, especially if it came from the pulpit in a Catholic Church, from a person they trusted to be teaching them the truth.

The most serious offenders, those punished by the Inquisition, were apostatizing under the official titles of Catholic priests, bishops and etc. They were brought before the Inquisition and given the choice to convert or leave the country. Many had been called in, had asked forgiveness, only to return to teaching heresy. And what with the shadow of those years of darkness still hovering over Spain, the State dealt with them, harshly.

In those days, there was no separation between Church and State, so a crime against the Church could be punished by the State. The function of the Church in the Inquisition was not to pass sentence; but to decide who was a heretic and who was not. Her focus was to correct error and stop its spread; the State saw these offenders as a threat to the country and acted accordingly. In no way are we excusing the abuses of the Inquisition, or the cruelty, at times. Any man's death is a crime against God, but so is the loss of one's soul. Once again, there were not good and bad guys; only weak frightened guys, tools of Satan and his lies.

Sixteenth Century and the war goes on!

Pope Leo X left a small crack in the door, and the enemy burst in, guns loaded! 1514, the year before Teresa was born, Pope Leo X granted an indulgence to faithful donating money toward the building of a new Basilica in Rome - St. Peter's Basilica. Although the indulgence called for the usual conditions of penance and contrition, it became highly controversial.

1515 - Teresa is born, and Martin Luther began his attack which will culminate with his assault on the very Foundations of the Catholic Church using the *selling of indulgences* as a weapon. As a result, not only would the Catholic world never be the same, but the very essence of Christianity would change for all time. Opening the door to more conflicts to this very day, this one act of disobedience was to lead to the scandal of (some say) over 40,000 splinters of the True Cross of Jesus. What with disobedience building on disobedience, and dissension on dissension, the unity Jesus prayed for, *"that all may be one as You, Father, are in Me, and I in You,"* instead became Christian against Christian, brother against brother, and how Our Lord weeps!

Again, we come to Our Lord Jesus and how He defends His Church. Reading the History of the Church, and researching the lives of the Saints, there can be no doubt that it is the Roman Catholic Church which was founded by Jesus. We can see Him, faithful God to an unfaithful people, fighting the enemy who is dedicated to destroying the Church, through chosen ones-such as Saint Teresa of Avila. We, as a Church, would have been dead long before we were 100 years old, if we had not been the Church which flowed from the very Heart of Jesus on the Cross! Heart from Heart, He has preserved us, watching over us till He comes again. The conclusion is irrefutable - we are the Church, the only Church founded by Jesus!

Teresa, Role Model for Catholics and non-Catholics

We would be foolish to believe it was merely a coincidence that Teresa was born the very year Martin Luther came out with his dogma *of salvation through grace alone.* Whereas Luther, confused by his conflict between the flesh and the spirit, addressed his dilemma by embracing the good things of the world,[11] condemning any law of the Church or part of Scripture which would restrict him; Teresa was to live a *radical* life of obedience, often under the worst of conditions, choosing the *Lord* of all, rather than the *all.*

Although Teresa was and is truly *Catholic*, she has been hailed as a powerful Role Model for non-Catholics as well. Crashaw, the English Protestant poet, who converted to Catholicism and later became a Priest, was just one of the many whose lives were changed as a result of her writings.

Saint Edith Stein went from being born a *Jewess*, to a life of science with the *exclusion of God*, to *conversion* to the Roman Catholic Church because of Saint Teresa's writings.

Macauley, a historian, said Teresa did more to block the spread of Protestantism, by her life and writings, than even St. Ignatius of Loyola, *"If St. Ignatius of Loyola is the brain of the Catholic reaction, Teresa is its heart; if Ignatius is the head of a great band, Teresa of Jesus belongs to its humanity."*[12]

Saints like Francis de Sales and Alphonsus Liguori, both Doctors of the Church, not only greatly admired her, but turned to her works for enlightenment and inspiration. She influenced the life of the great mystic and Doctor of the Church - St. John of the Cross. Her autobiography, reluctantly written, out of obedience to her Spiritual Director, has been praised as one of the most important books on the *Christian Way of Life.*

Always obedient, Teresa burned her books! During one of the Inquisitions, at which she had to answer questions on her

---

[11]according to the world's values
[12]Saint Teresa of Avila, William Thomas Walsh - TAN Publishers

visions, she was ordered to burn all her writings; and she did! If
her Nuns, without her knowledge, had not copied the books, the
Church would not have the wealth of knowledge infused into her
by the Holy Spirit, and she would not have been awarded the
title: *Doctor of the Church.*

Popes, over the centuries, have extolled St. Teresa and her
writings. **Pope St. Pius X** said one need go no farther than her
books to discover how to live a truly holy life; that in her works
she very clearly directs one, from the very ordinary, everyday
living of the Christian life, to the highest peaks of holiness. Very
simply, she teaches that true progress in prayer is achieved by the
faithful fulfilling of our daily duties with Christ as the center, and
the living out of our belief in a holy and obedient manner.

God plants Teresa in good soil, a holy family will nourish.

Teresa was groomed by God for her mission; He not only
infused His Divine Knowledge into her through the Holy Spirit;
but meticulously prepared his little charge. God leaving nothing
to chance, had her descend from the *Ahumados*, mighty crusaders
against the Moors. From an early age, she wanted to be a martyr
for the Faith; she and her brother Rodrigo even tried, as little
children, to go to the East to die a Martyr's death at the hands of
the Moors.

Unlike Luther who came from an abusive family and later
said he was terrified of his parents, Teresa wrote that she was her
father's favorite and her parents were virtuous and charitable to
those who were less fortunate than they. She said that she never
heard a harsh word uttered in her family, toward her, or any of
the children.

Luther told his father, he became a priest because he was
afraid God would strike him down, if he did not; on the other
hand, Teresa, filled with the stories of Saints her family had
shared with her, loved her Lord so, she could not bear to be
separated from him, even suffering the worst pain when leaving
her father. When she presented her desire to become a Nun to
her father, he replied, emphatically: *"No, definitely no! Should*

you so desire after I am dead, so be it."
   She was upset, as she did not want to hurt her father. But afraid she might weaken in her resolve, she quickly ran to the Convent of the Incarnation of the Carmelite Nuns outside of Avila. She recalls, *"while leaving my father's house, I knew I would not, even at the very moment and agony of my death, feel the anguish of separation more painfully than at that point in time, not even the love of God I had inside me could make up for the love I felt for my father and friends."*

The long dark night of the soul
   For twenty years, from ages twenty four to forty four, Teresa was to know *Purgatory on Earth*. Like most Saints whom the Lord chooses, she had very poor health. More dead than alive for most her life, her physical pains were joined by spiritual and mental ones. One time, the Nuns thought she had died and they wanted to bury her; there was not a sign of life; but because of Teresa's father's insistence they did not; and she awakened days later, after a lit candle spilled over on her rousing her from a deep coma.
   In the painful journey from sinner to Saint,[13] Teresa shares the lonely walk through the *"dark night of the soul,"* where you turn your back on all you have known, all the little delights of this world, to soar to that unity, that *oneness* with the Lord. Being put to the test, as our Lord is prone to do for those who ask for a deeper relationship with Him, Teresa was to fall over and over again. But she did not blame anyone; she got up again, soldier that she was to fight another day!
   Her walk was not easy; she had an ongoing struggle between the tugging of the world-her family and friends, and the gentle tugging at her heart by Jesus. Around 1555, someone brought a painting to the Convent, Our Savior bleeding, bruised, His back swollen- scarred by huge gaping wounds, resulting from His flagellation. He looked so young, His Eyes so hurt, she

---

[13]Teresa often called herself a terrible sinner

prostrated herself before her beloved Spouse, and begged Him to release her from the enticements of the world and enslavement of the flesh. She asked His forgiveness for the many times she had foolishly been tempted by people and things, crying out, *"My Lord and my God, I will not get up from here until you grant me this favor."*

This was the turning point in Teresa's life. She had passionately prayed with all her heart, and the Savior answered her. She had fought the good fight and won! She was free, free at last of the seductions of the devil and his kingdom-the world. She never forgot this Image of Her suffering Lord and carried a statue of Jesus at the Pillar with her, as she went about opening house after house.[14]

Luther could not stand to look upon the suffering Jesus; he wrote: *"I was such an enemy of Christ on His Cross, I loathed the sight and shut my eyes and felt that I would have rather seen the devil."* Luther took Jesus off the Cross. What Satan could not do when he taunted Jesus to come down from the Cross, one of Jesus' beloved, trusted sons would do. As a young seminarian he was so traumatized by excessive scrupulosity, he turned against the very sign in our lives of the price paid for our salvation-Our Crucified Lord.

Teresa fought the temptations of the world; Luther gave in to them. Teresa chose the Primitive Rule of Carmel,[15] the strictest rule in the Church, which stated, in addition to the vows of poverty, chastity and obedience, *"the Nuns were to maintain complete silence at certain hours; to remain in their cells meditating on their God when not busy with other tasks; to fast from September 14, the Exaltation of the Cross to Easter, unless physically unable; to eat no meat (unless it was required because of health reasons); be engaged in doing all sorts of physical work for the Community."*

---

[14]all seventeen
[15]formed by St. Albert in 1209

Teresa was adopting a Rule which encompassed *"the Exaltation of the Cross,"* teaching her Nuns, and the Church at large,[16] that it is through the Holy Cross that we have Redemption; it is because of Good Friday that we have Easter Sunday; it is through suffering that we get to *truly* know the Savior. Meditating on the Cross and His Passion, filled Teresa with such love for the Lord, He could reach deep into her heart and soul, making her one with Him.

He needed balm for His wounded Heart. He loved her so, one night He sent an Angel who pierced her heart with an arrow, that her heart might know the Passion and Love which His Heart knew when It was pierced out of love for her and us. The Lord trusted her with His Love and His mission, and she proved herself worthy of that trust.

She spoke of sacrifice, dying to self! Luther, because he fell victim to self-will and self-indulgence not only sinned against his vows, he led others to do so. Oh, Luther, what could God have done through you, if only you had obeyed the descendant of the Rock upon which He built His Church? Luther lamented, as he prepared to face the Father, that he had tried to get rid of *one* Pope and he ended up creating *one hundred.* We who have inherited this madness, see Christians spending precious years arguing over what - we know not, dissent causing disharmony, disharmony creating dispute, dispute bringing about division, until we are no longer the Body of Christ, but lambs being led to slaughter. Along with Teresa, we cry out Jesus' plea,

"Come back to me, with all your heart
Don't let fear keep us apart
Long have I waited for your coming home to Me
And living deeply our new life
The wilderness will lead you
To your heart, where I will speak

---

[16]As a Doctor of the Church, her writings are taught to future priests and are approved teachings of the Church.

*Long have I waited for your coming home to Me
And living deeply our new life."*[17]

Jesus told us that *"For whoever wishes to save his life will lose it, but whoever loses his life for My sake and that of the Gospel will save it."*[18] Luther thought of the *todays* in his life and forgot the *tomorrows*. Teresa lived her whole life with her eyes on the Kingdom, living for her Lord, following the Gospel life by obeying first her Lord and then all those in authority, representing Him on earth-the Holy See and his apostles. Her eyes on the world to come, not this temporary, passing world of illusions, she walked through fire, her Lord by her side to comfort her and guide her. For *twenty years* she was to go through the worst battles, falling and getting up, then falling all over again. When she recalled the Lord's many gifts to her, and the price He paid to ransom her and us from death, she grieved all the more for allowing herself to be drawn away from Him and their life together. *But she tried!* She struggled, *every day of her life*, for a closer and more intimate relationship with her Lord. *She tried!*

The devil never leaves her alone; Teresa doubts her visions

Suddenly a fear ran through the villages and cities-The Inquisition! It had been years since anyone had thought about the Inquisition. The Inquisition which had begun under King Ferdinand and Queen Isabella had laid dormant under Charles the Fifth. Now it was suddenly reinstated, because of an incident which was to erupt covering many lives and souls, and worse bring fear into the hearts of the people.

There was a Nun, Magdalena de la Cruz, whose reputation as a faster, mystic and stigmatist reached all of Spain, even gaining the attention and respect of the Crown. Word spread of her gifts of healings and the faithful came from far and near, to ask for her prayers, taking back with them objects she had

---

[17]excerpts from the album *"Listen,"*-copyright 1972 Benedictine Foundation of the State of Vermont Inc. Weston Priory, Weston, VT
[18]Mk 8:35

touched, as relics. Members of the *royal family* held her in such high regard, they would ask her to pray for them and intercede with our Lord Jesus for them. Now, if all the notoriety, fame and adulation she received was not enough, the Nun (Satan and his pride) let it be known that she lived strictly on the Consecrated Host, requiring no other nourishment to sustain life. The Inquisition, becoming suspicious, arrested and questioned Magdalena, whereupon she made a confession so diabolical that it lead to her imprisonment. She told the inquisitors in Cordoba that she was not a Catholic, but an *Alumbrada*, a secret sect exposed a generation before by the Inquisition. It was an anti-Christian secret society which had been crippling Europe by undermining Christ's teachings and His Call for unity under the one true Cross.

She confessed to being a devil-worshiper, and that she had been induced by the devil, at seven years of age, to *feign* the wounds of the Stigmata. At eleven, with the help of two demons who visited her periodically, she had administered the wounds on her hands, feet and side, imitating the Wounds of Our Beloved Lord Jesus.[19] She recounted how she had become quite adept at affecting trances where she became impervious to the pricks of needles and other forms of testing. She had been able to deceive everyone into believing she lived only on the Sacred Host[20] for *twelve years*, until one day food was discovered hidden in her cell at the Convent.

As incredulous as it may seem, although everyone who ever met Teresa could plainly see she was humble and sincere, *she* soon fell under suspicion. Townspeople began to whisper she was like Magdalena de la Cruz. The problem with false

---

[19]There have been genuine Stigmatists in our Church, like St. Francis of Assisi, and Padre Pio, who bore the wounds of Christ on their bodies.

[20]There have been many documented accounts of Eucharistic Fasters, people who lived on no food other than the Eucharist for periods of up to 35 years. See chapter on Eucharistic Saints and Fasters, *This Is My Body, This Is My Blood, Miracles of the Eucharist.*

mystics like Magdalena is that they could very cleverly imitate the outward signs of a true mystic like Teresa. Although Teresa was long free from any need to receive approval from the world, she began to *doubt* her gifts, to believe the townspeople might be right. *Suppose she had been deceived by the evil one!* She brought this fear to a Priest she highly respected. This questioning of herself alone, should have been proof she was not an Alumbrada, as they were hardly known for any type of humility or sincerity.

Her friends, who *loved* her, began to conjecture on whether Teresa's gifts were from God or the devil. A person whose opinions she valued, suggested she seek spiritual advice from an exemplary Priest known for his love of the Blessed Sacrament and for bringing many back to the Church. He was reputed to be a truly dependable and holy Priest. Because of her humility, and always striving for perfection, she confessed what she called *her terrible imperfections.* The Priest, concluding the Lord would not give favors, such as she spoke of, to someone with all her faults, ordered her to give up all forms of *Mental Prayer.*

She shared what the Priest had said, with her friend Maestro Daza, seeking his counsel while at the same time enjoining him to keep all she had confided *secret.* In an effort to help her, he asked advice of friends, recounting the Priest's verdict, inadvertently spreading doubts about Teresa. The Priest's evaluation of Teresa's Visions coming from diabolical sources, *spread* throughout Avila. The Priest, along with another holy and learned man, confident her *Mental Prayer* was all the work of the devil, advised her to go and give an account of her whole life to a Priest of the Company of Jesus,[21] *"as she was in*

---

[21]It is interesting to note that the Company of Jesus' founder, St. Ignatius who, with a band of nine companions set out for Rome to seek permission from the Pope to serve God and their fellow men, was once looked upon as a heretic and arrested by the Inquisition at Alcalá. Exonerated, he and his company went on to preach the Word and tend to the poor throughout

much peril."

As Teresa was growing deeper and deeper in her journey with the Lord, she went about her everyday life, fully living out her commitment to her vocation as a Nun, as well as to her *immediate* family. But this was to become a time of struggle of the worst kind, a time when she was to suffer one of her most painful temptations. She was plagued with doubts she had never had before: that her mystical experiences might be the work and deception of the devil. She had no peace until a holy confessor, who understood her type of spirituality, assured her they were of God.

Teresa comes under suspicion once again

People who held high positions in the Church, were exposed as Lutherans![22] They read like a *"Who's Who of Spain,"* including the clergy, a bishop who had been slated to become Archbishop of Toledo, many of Spain's most influential citizens. Priests and Nuns considered holy, confessed that they had spread dangerous heresies. King Philip called a state of emergency. He had to nip an impending disturbance in the bud; the Church had become fractured by this false mystic, Maria Magdalena de la Cruz, and the divisions could have split the church and the country, apart. The King decided to take matters into his own hands and call for an Inquisition!

There was a madness running wild in the streets, an anger; they had been betrayed; they had loved having a holy person to go to, to touch, to intercede for them with God; remember they had been centuries without much knowledge of the Faith. They didn't know if they were angry with Magdalena or with the Church for exposing her.

Italy, Spain and France. The Jesuits have been attributed with the renewal of devotion to the Holy Eucharist. Pope St. Pius X declared they had been called to bring new life to The Catholic Church, through the faithful's frequent reception of the Sacraments of Confession and Communion.

[22]Lutherans, Calvinists, Unitarians, even Catholics who were not friendly to the Church were called *Lutherans* by Teresa.

Defenders of the Faith

Everyone became suspect. Teresa was again deserted by friends; her confessors kept grilling her over and over again; her visions were probed and her heart pierced; she was either harassed or avoided. Isolated, abandoned, she was even denied the comfort and companionship of her books, as books not written in Latin were under suspicion, because of translations that were not authentic and heretics *misusing* books to spread heresy. As Teresa did not know how to read Latin, and all her favorite books written in the vernacular (Spanish), were now forbidden, she felt quite alone! Even *St. Jerome's Epistles*, the *Confessions of St. Augustine*, and *The Imitation of Christ, written in the vernacular*,²³ were on the condemned list. One day, all alone and weary, she heard the voice of Christ, *"Never mind I will give you a living book."*

She was not only to be deprived of reading religious books, her Confessor forbid her to receive her Precious Lord in Holy Communion, day after day, for nearly three weeks. Censured, accused, slandered, deprived of her only consolation, Holy Communion, she felt abandoned, even by God. The Confessor continued to order Teresa to rebuke the Visions. Although agonizing, her head and heart pounding, she obeyed; she even *obeyed* when he ordered her to throw Holy Water on the Vision of our Lord.

She said, *"This gave me the greatest sorrow for I could not believe it was not God. And although they ordered me to send Him away, I could not bear Him leaving me."* The Lord told her not to worry, that she did well to obey. One day, after suffering one of her worst trials, she felt the Presence of Jesus; she said she could see Him with the eyes of her heart. Fighting back the tears, but too weak to do anything but obey her Confessor, she held up her Crucifix, so that if it was in truth, the devil, as her confessor insisted, he would disappear. Instead, Our Lord appeared to her; He was radiant; more beautiful than

---

²³the latin versions were not forbidden reading.

anything or anyone she had ever seen. He came toward her; then he extended His Hand, gently took the Crucifix from her and returned it: *"When He gave it back to me, it was of four large stones, much more precious, beyond compare, than diamonds. It had the five wounds very exquisitely wrought."* He told Teresa that was how she would see it from now on, but she alone.

Teresa's words speak so eloquently of the life of a Saint on earth, misunderstood, persecuted, accused, deserted, tortured, but always trusting in the Lord, glorifying *His Name*.

Teresa had no patience with people saying *The devil made me do it.* She felt that they were not accepting responsibility for their actions. Surely, she believed in the devil; she had had her own experiences with him, but she also knew his limitations, and this she imparted to her Nuns:

"The devil! The devil! where we could say, 'God! God!' and make him tremble. Yes, for we know he cannot even move unless the Lord permits it. What is this? There is no doubt that I am more afraid of those who are so afraid of the devil than I am of him, for he can't do anything to me, and they, especially if they are Confessors, disturb me much, and I have spent several years in such great trouble, that now I wonder how I have been able to endure it. Blessed be the Lord, Who has so truly helped me."

The Lord had finally freed her from fear, but not from persecution. The Inquisition continued to hang ominously over her head.

Teresa has a visit from the devil

When Teresa would go into rapture or ecstasy, she would be so enraptured by the Lord she would levitate! But her ecstasies were not always uninterrupted bliss. This one time, on the eve of All Souls Day when Teresa was in particular praying for the Poor Souls in Purgatory, who should appear to harass her, and interrupt her prayers but the *slimy one.* The devil would not leave; she took holy water and doused him with it, and he immediately disappeared. [Holy water is a Sacramental and the devil hates it, as he does all Sacramentals like the Rosary, the Scapular, the Sign of the Cross, candles, priests' vestments, blessed ashes on Ash Wednesday.] No sooner had the devil disappeared, Teresa saw souls leaving Purgatory.

Another time, a black creature came beside her; he was snarling like a mad dog, furious because she was bringing about reform in the Carmelite Order. At first she laughed at his attempts to frighten her. Even after he began beating her brutally on the head, arms and legs, she continued to laugh so as to not alarm the nuns with her. As they had not seen the creature, she did not want to alarm them, so she did not ask them for holy water. But the pain got so unbearable she did ask. They doused her with holy water; but he did not stop beating her! His roar becoming louder and louder, she grabbed the holy water, and threw it on him disdainfully, without fear; and he disappeared, at last!

It was stories like this that gave a confessor and a Spiritual Director, lacking experience in the mystical life, cause to wonder, or at best think, if he is losing his mind. Even friends of Teresa suggested that Teresa be exorcised!

Times were dire, once again. It was 1559, the King of Spain was ill and looking feeble; he spent his last days getting the throne in readiness for his son, Philip II. The Duke of Alba marched on Rome and humbled Pope Paul IV. With a grand army he had rounded up, Philip dealt a crushing defeat on the French in their back yard. He had always desired to bring England back to the Catholic Church. Now Philip II, King of Spain was married to Mary Tudor! He had lost his opportunity to be emperor, but as Mary's spouse, he hoped to unite Spain and England, with the intention of restoring England to the Catholic Church. He was committed to undo the harm that Luther and Calvin had brought about and unite all Christendom under the one true Cross, and the Chair of Peter. With all Christians united, and strong because of that unity, the splinters having returned to the Faith, he could forestall a Moslem invasion which was always hanging over the sovereign's head like the sword of Damocles. It was no small threat, as the followers of Islam had invaded the coasts of Italy and taken Tripoli.

There was only one problem, his wife died! At first, he entertained the idea of marrying Elizabeth I of England; but the powerful Calvinists in charge of her cabinet immediately took over and heavily influenced her against the Church and Philip. His plans to unite England never came to pass. In addition, the Emperor made a shocking discovery, while he and his son were off fighting, defending the Church in foreign kingdoms against Calvinism, this heretical force was infiltrating Spain.

He reopened the Inquisition with the express order, to seek out the perpetrators, call them before the Inquisition, and if they did not recant all they had taught and promise to cease from teaching heresies in the future, to exile them or put them to death. They discovered conspiracies among the most trusted clergy and members of the court plotting against the Church. Even his wife's confessor, the soon to be Archbishop of Toledo, after much investigation, was found to be teaching the views and heresies of Luther and was called before the Inquisition. Men in high places were found guilty of apostasy. One, an eloquent speaker in the Royal court was found to be not only a Lutheran and guilty of heresy, but he confessed to being a bigamist! He committed suicide in prison.

In Valladolid, the Lutherans had been openly holding meetings at the home of Don Agustín Cazalla, who was not only a priest, but one of the King's most trusted chaplains. He had in addition a doctorate and was a highly respected professor at the university. He was found not only guilty of being a Lutheran but it came out that the learned priest - Doctor Cazalla, was a descendant of a family committed to destroying the Church. Their clandestine adventures to undermine the teachings of the Church were what brought about the *first* Spanish Inquisition. The priest had never divulged this connection.

To those who believe, the means used were too severe, let

us quote from one of the heretics: *"If they had waited four months to persecute us, we should have been as many as they; and in six months we should have done to them what they are doing to us."*[24]

Historians believe that had Philip II not acted swiftly, Spain would have suffered the same bloodshed, the endless internal struggles, the devastating civil wars, separating and nearly ruining France and the horrific Thirty Years Wars which razed Germany and nearly destroyed her, Germany split till today between Lutherans and Catholics.

As Philip was still in the Nordic nations,[25] he delegated the responsibility to Princess Juana, his sister. It's reported that she, Don Carlos (heir to the throne) and Don Juan of Austria were present at one of the bloodiest spectacles Spain had witnessed in years. Emotions ran high! Some people felt betrayed and used this opportunity to see justice done, forgetting that Justice is the Lord's and only He had the right to mete it out; and then others were there, like the pagans of Ancient Rome, just to see a show.

There were more than 200,000 spectators crowding the sides of the road waiting to behold the fallen illustrious, solemnly processing by. It would have been almost impossible to separate those faithful to the crown and the Church, from those who were not; if not for the fact that the guilty were walking in the back of the procession, wearing yellow *sanbenitos*.[26]

Now when these heretics had gone before the Inquisitors,

---

[24]p.142, Saint Teresa of Avila, William Thomas Walsh - TAN Publishers

[25]the Scandinavian countries

[26]*San Benito* is Spanish for St. Benedict. The *sanbenito* was a garment, resembling the scapular of St. Benedict, which covered the front and the back of the wearer. During the Spanish Inquisition, confessed heretics wore a yellow *sanbenito* with a St. Andrew's red cross on the front and on the back of the scapular. When they were condemned and were approaching execution as heretics and enemies of the state they wore black *sanbenitos* with flames and devils, etc. in place of the Cross. Webster's Dictionary - Simon and Schuster

they were given an opportunity to explain the circumstances around their falling into error, and repent. Sixteen did so and were reconciled with Mother Church and released. The fourteen who were now filing past had refused to repent. They were found to be heretics, and the Inquisition had found no recourse but to hand them over to the Royal Court. As the heretics were considered dangerous because of their positions, a threat to the state, and as heresy was considered an act of high treason, it fell to the state to pass sentence and bring about the execution of the guilty.

It was so sad to see priests and nuns, knights of the Court, a judge and even women who had been so deluded they chose to attempt to undermine the Church and consequently the state. The nuns had been respected and looked upon as holy and therefore Role Models to young women entertaining a religious life; imagine the hurts, the dead souls of those whom they had betrayed. In Seville, heresies and heretics had crept into the monasteries, firmly entrenching themselves in the cloisters, spreading its poison among the religious. Then it spilled into the streets, to the laity. In Seville, fifty were burned at the stake, including a Dominican formerly looked upon as holy and virtuous, when he was discovered secretly teaching contrary to the Faith and distributing books written in Spanish on Lutheranism.

Once a fire is lit, the smoke often takes centuries to clear. It went on and on, with neighbor accusing neighbor, a lineup of the most respected (and envied?) standing before the Royal court. Heretics were being reported in different areas in Spain; it became almost like a Salem witch hunt. The problem was that those who were finally executed would not pledge obedience to the one true Faith. And then there were those who had feigned repentance at previous Inquisitions, made a vow to teach only the Magisterium, then reneged and continued to teach the same heresies.

Teresa is accused and called *again* before the Inquisition!

Now you remember Doctor Cazalla! Well the condemned heretic had been preaching in Avila! Now the talk around Avila was, Was Teresa part of the heretics who were invading the minds and souls of Spain? Before you knew it, the wagging tongues of people, who had nothing better to do than gossip, spread scandal and doubt about Teresa.

This Saint, suffered an endless hell on earth, because of the aftermath of fear and confusion resulting from the damage down by heretics and their apostatizing.

She did not condemn those who accused her of being a *Heretic*, a *Lutheran*, an *Illuminati*, an *Alumbrada*, a *devil-worshiper* and whatever else they could conjure up in their minds. She prayed for those who maligned her, interrogated her into the wee hours of the night, day in and day out. She bore no ill feelings toward those who had abandoned her, those fair-weather friends (as with Jesus when He walked the earth) who were at her side when she was well-accepted but left her when she was to be condemned. I guess her deepest wounds came from those who had no guile and truly believed her visions were from the devil; but she did not condemn them; instead, she grieved for them.

She did not even condemn the *heretics* who were burning Catholic churches, leading the innocent astray, killing Priests and Nuns, and desecrating the Body and Blood of Christ in His Blessed Sacrament. Although she did everything that she could, to protect the *Blessed Sacrament* from heretics who would harm her Jesus Who she knew was alive in the Eucharist, and no less alive than when He walked the earth. She always made sure to secure a safe place for the Blessed Sacrament before setting up the house that she was opening, for her nuns.

Out of love for Jesus, Who does not desire the death of a sinner but that he convert and be saved, she prayed for heretics; as they were baptized Catholics and therefore accountable, and as baptized Catholics she feared their souls would be lost. She did all sorts of penance for them, looking upon them as *victims* of a great lie, rather than as perpetrators.

Teresa - Crazy over the Eucharist

Saint Teresa was called, *"loca por la Eucaristía,"* crazy over the Eucharist. Like the Prophets, before and after her, Teresa believed God wants to speak to His children. But she knew that He tends to disguise Himself as a burning bush, at times in the wind, and Incarnate in Man. She was in love with This *God made Man,* but knew since the Ascension He could be found (physically) only in the Tabernacle. Teresa received her greatest graces after Communion and instructed her Nuns that the best time to spend with the Lord was right after Communion.

"The Lord had implanted such strong faith in her, that when she heard people saying they would like to have lived when Jesus was on earth, she used to smile because she regarded Him as being just as Present in the Blessed Sacrament as He had been then; so what difference did it make?"[27]

Teresa would ask for the largest Host, as that would take her longer to consume It; in that way, she would have her Lord with her longer. For two years Teresa had visions of Our Lord Jesus Christ. He would appear as the Risen Christ in the consecrated Host, when all was going well for her; then He would talk to her sweetly, gently. Then at other times, when she felt all alone and abandoned, He would come to her, speak to her firmly; but with compassion shining in His Eyes, sharing *His Pain,* uniting it with *her pain.*

But when she was knowing the greatest tribulation, afraid she felt that she could not get up one more time, He would appear to her sweating blood and tears in the Garden, or being scourged on the Pillar, or being humiliated as He is receiving the Crown of thorns, or bent over from under the weight of the Cross as He is carrying it to Golgotha, or finally mercifully dying - his wounded Body not able to give anymore love, with that last

---

[27]*cf*Teresa's Way of Perfection - 34,6

ounce of Love, dying for us on the Cross. When she had those visions, then she could love with His Heart, open her arms to more rejection, her eyes to more horror, her ears to more hatred and love her fellow men, because He loved them before her. But recounting them to her confessors, under obedience, caused her more rejection and wounding judgments.

Teresa and her love for God the Father - the One she loved
Teresa had had a wonderful relationship with her earthly father. But the love and relationship she had with God the Father was unique onto its own. Teresa discovered a *new image* of the Almighty Father. As well as her *Omnipotent* God, the *Divine Father* Who gave His only Son up to death for her, she saw Him as a *concerned* Father, a *loving* Father involved in the affairs of men, and a *caring* Father by her side, with her, amongst the pots and pans. She discovered Him hidden, too, within the *castle* of each person's soul. She found God the Father so touchable, so approachable, so within reach that she described *prayer as talking to God.* When trying to define her walk with the Lord, she said simply, *"Mental prayer is nothing else, in my opinion, but friendly conversation with Someone who loves us."*

Teresa - at last, at last a daughter of the Church!
Teresa discovered her Church, *in* all her glory, *through* all the Church's dignity, *as Bride of Christ.* But to her sadness, she found this Church she loved so very much, besieged by great evils, as well. She never raised her voice against the hierarchy or rebel over the injustices she endured, but remained faithful and obedient, *a daughter of the Church.* She imparted this to her Nuns, as well. She said their call was to surround themselves with simplicity, to thirst for poverty, to be a reflection of *Christ among them,* in their cheerfulness and joy. They were to pray for all defenders of the Church. *And by their life, to be the light, the salt, the leaven from which the world would rise from the depths to be lifted up on high with the Savior.*
I think the single greatest trait, outside of her passion for

Jesus, was her sincere and consistent humility. Humility is not weakness, helplessly standing by and letting God do it. Teresa knew that God raised certain people to defend His Church and to address the wrongs; and that she did, but always obedient to the Church, deferring to the authority of the Vicar of Christ. Teresa was well aware, *in her time,* of the attitudes of the men of the Church and she responded by praying to her Lord,

"When you walked on this earth, Lord, you did not despise women; rather you always helped them and showed great compassion toward them. And you found as much love and more faith in them than you did in men. Among them was your Most Blessed Mother, and through her merits we merit what, because of our offenses, we do not deserve."

Till the end, Jesus and her Love, the Blessed Sacrament

According to her nurse, Teresa asked for the Blessed Sacrament. When they were taking the Lord away, she sat up in bed with a great surge of spirit and said joyfully:

"My Lord, it is time to be going. Very well, Your Will be done."

On the 4th of October, 1582, at sixty seven years old, she closed her eyes for the last time. Her last words,

"A daughter of the Church; at last a daughter of the Church."

✞✞✞

Let nothing disturb you
Let nothing frighten you
All things pass away:
God never changes.
Patience obtains all things.
He who has God
finds he lacks nothing
God alone suffices.

Teresa de Jesús [28]

---

[28]Many quotes and information was taken from either Saint Teresa's *Life* or Bob and Penny Lord's chapter on Teresa in their book: *"Saints and other Powerful Women in the Church."*

Bibliography

Defenders of the Faith - Super Saints Book III

Butler, Alban Rev. - *Lives of the Fathers,*
        Martyrs and other Saints
    Volumes I-II-III - J. Sadlier Co, Boston 1833
Butler, Thurston & Atwater - *Lives of the Saints*
    Complete edition in 4 volumes - Christian Classics
    Westminster, Maryland 1980
Plassman Thomas Fr. OFM - Vann, Joseph Fr. OFM
    Lives of the Saints - John J. Crawley New York 1953
Tylenda, Joseph N. SJ - *Jesuit Saints & Martyrs*
    Loyola University Press - Chicago, IL 1983
Courtois Gaston Abbé - *St. Vincent de Paul*
    Editions Pleurus, Paris France 1950
Genelli, Fr. SJ - *Life of St. Ignatius of Loyola*
    Tan Publishers - Rockford, IL - 1988
Cerri, Oreste - *S. Filippo Neri*
    Il Villaggio Fanciullo di Vergiate, Italy 1939
Walsh, William Thomas - *St. Teresa of Avila*
    Tan Publications, Rockford, IL - 1987

Index

Alter Christus, 95
Angel Gabriel, 57
Angelic intercessions, 97
Angels, 29
Ann Boleyn, 124
Ann of Austria, 60
Annecy, France, 30
Apostle of the Chablais, 46
Apostle of the Laity, 17
Apparitions of Our Lady, 97
Autun, France, 55
Beatification of St. Francis de Sales, 49
Blessed Mother, 11, 14, 85, 175
Blessed Sacrament, 219
Burgundy, district of, 53
Calvin, 12
Calvinism, 39, 53, 77
Cardinal Alessandrino, 133
Cardinal Giovanni Medici, 129
Carmelite Order, 212
Catechism for the Catholic Church, 139
Catherine of Aragon, 139
Catholic Queen and King, Isabella and Ferdinand, 138, 165
Chablais, duchy of, 39
Chair of Peter, 212
Chapel of the Holy Crib, 187
Company of Jesus, 176, 185
Council in Mantova, 125
Council of Trent, 99, 102, 105, 119, 126
Counter-Reformation, 97, 119, 165, 195
Countess Joiguy, 73
Congregation for the Doctrine of the Faith, 146
Congregation of the Visitation of the Virgin Mary, 57
Counter-Reformation, 9, 11
Dames of the Cross, 91
Daughters of Charity, 75
Demons, 20
Descendants of Peter, 119
Doctrine of Transubstantiation, 103
Edict of Worms, 122
Elizabeth I of England, 134
Emperor Charles I, 122
Emperor Charles V, 126
First Holy Communion, 30
Garden of Eden, 9
Gift of Prophecy, 22
Granting of indulgences, 121
Grand Sultan, 69
Gulf of Lepanto, 143
Henry Cardinal Newman, 100
Henry VIII, 97, 124
Heresy of Albigensianism, 61
Holy Coincidence, 30
Holy Family, 35
Holy House of Loreto, 35
Holy Land, 177
Holy Roman Empire, 125
House of Savoie, 39
Inquisition, 128, 134, 183, 207
Inquisition in Spain, 137, 198
Introduction to a Devout Life, 47
Islam, 69
Jansenius, 92
Jesus Crucified, 175
John Calvin, 29, 97, 115, 129
Justification through Faith, 9
King Ferdinand and Queen Isabella, 198
King Louis XIII, 83, 85, 89
King Louis XV, 91
Lake Annecy, 59
Lake Geneva, 43
Lake Maggiore, 98
Lazarites or Lazarians, 83
Little Office of the Blessed Virgin, 175
Lutheranism, 61, 122
Luther, 9, 12, 97, 196, 205
Magdalena de la Cruz, 206
Medici family, 121
Miracles of the Eucharist, 97
Missionaries of St. Francis de Sales, 50

Mohammed, 70
Monte Cassino, 14
Moslem, 138
Mother Mary, 9, 29
Mystical Body of
Christ, 17
New World, 11
Oblates of St. Francis
de Sales, 50
Oliver Cromwell, 97
One World Order, 12
Papal Bull in 1570, 140
Patron Saint of
Journalists, 49
Original Sin, 63
Pippo Bono, 13
Pope Alexander VII, 84
Pope Clement VII,
123, 124
Pope Clement VIII, 26,
43, 44
Pope Clement XII, 94
Pope Gregory XIII, 26
Pope Gregory XIV, 22,
26
Pope Gregory XV, 28
Pope Hadrian VI, 121
Pope John Paul II, 131,
148, 195
Pope John XXIII, 130
Pope Julius II, 120
Pope Julius III, 103,
104, 126
Pope Leo X, 120, 121,
200
Pope Marcellus II, 127
Pope Paul III, 99, 124,
126, 130, 188
Pope Pius IV, 26, 98,
128100, 103, 104, 105
Pope St. Pius V, 9, 26,
97, 108, 120, 132, 136

Pope St. Pius X, 202
Pope Pius XI, 49
Pope Urban VIII, 83
Primitive Rule of
Carmel, 204
Protestant
Reformation, 119, 138
Renaissance, 12, 117
Richilieu, 89
Rosary Crusade, 143
Sacrament of Baptism,
19
Sacrament of
Confirmation, 19
Sacrament of Extreme
Unction, 19
Sacrament of Holy
Orders, 19, 31
Sacrament of
Matrimony, 19
Sacraments, 19
Sacraments of
Reconciliation and
Holy Communio, 19
Sacraments of the
Church, 54
Sacrifice of the Cross,
18
Sacrifice of the Mass,
11
Saint of the
Earthquake, 16
Saints of the Counter-
Reformation, 49
Salesian Order, 50
Saracens, 165
Satan, 168
Seven churches of
Rome, 15
Salesian Order, 50
Society of Jesus, 97,
165, 188

Society of the Oratory,
74
Spiritual Exercises, 180
Solomon, 54
Spotless Vessel, 9
St. Augustine, 47, 108
St. Catherine dei Ricci,
9
St. Charles Borromeo,
9, 26, 44, 105
St. Charles Borromeo,
44
St. Edith Stein, 197
St. Francis de Sales, 9,
54
St. Ignatius of Loyola,
9, 26
St. Jane Frances de
Chantal, 9
St. John Bosco, 50
St. John Chrysostom,
145
St. John Fisher, 9
St. John of the Cross, 9
St. Louise de Marillac,
75
St. Paschal Baylon, 165
St. Paul, 47
St. Peter's Basilica, 200
St. Philip Neri, 9
St. Robert Bellarmine,
9, 43
St. Teresa of Avila, 9,
200
St. Thomas Aquinas,
108
St. Thomas More, 9
St. Vincent de Paul, 9
Sultan Mohammed II,
141
Vatican Council II, 131
Switzerland, 29

Videos available based on this book

V120
Saint Philip Neri

St. Philip Neri

Bob& Penny Lord

Walk the streets of Rome where **St. Philip Neri** began his ministry. Follow him as he teaches the brothers, who are now the Oratorians. Visit **Chiesa Nuova,** the Church where he lived, died, experienced **Ecstasy, Our Lady appeared** to him and where **Pope John Paul II** went to honor him.

V121 - Sts. Francis de Sales & Frances de Chantal

St. Francis de Sales & St. Jane Francis de Chantal

Bob& Penny Lord

Visit the shrines of **St. Francis de Sales and St. Jane Frances Chantal, in Annecy, France**, nestled deep in the **French Alps.** Visit his **chateau** which is still inhabited by members of his family. Go to the majestic church of the **Visitation,** protecting the town, where both Saints are buried.

V136
St. Vincent de Paul

St. Vincent de Paul

Bob& Penny Lord

One of *the most powerful* Saints of France. Go to **Paris** and the Chapel of the **Miraculous Medal,** where his **incorrupt heart** is venerated. Go to the Church of **St. Vincent de Paul** where his life story is recounted in stained glass windows and where his **incorrupt body** is visible.

V153
Saint Charles Borromeo

St. Charles Borromeo

Bob& Penny Lord

Begin in Arona, birthplace of St. Charles. On to Pavia, where he attended the University, then to Trent where he worked on the Council of Trent, to Rome and to Milan where he was Archbishop. Visit the Cathedral in Milan where he is buried.

V162
Saint Ignatius of Loyola

St. Ignatius of Loyola

Bob& Penny Lord

Founder of the Jesuits born in Loyola, Spain at the foot of the Pyrenees. Originally a soldier, he threw down his sword to serve the Lord. He took his first vows in Montmartre in Paris, was ordained in Rome and took vows in St. Paul outside the Walls. He died in 1556 and is buried in the Gesu in Rome.

V143
St. Teresa of Avila

St. Teresa of Avila

Bob& Penny Lord

Mystic - Doctor of the Church - Reformer of the Carmelite Order Avila - Visit house where St. Teresa was born and the cell where she received **Transverberation of the heart. Alba de Tormes** - Where she died. See her tomb, her **incorrupt arm** and her **incorrupt heart.**

Produced by Journeys of Faith®
To Order call 1-800-633-2484

Journeys of Faith®

To Order: 1-800-633-2484 FAX 916-853-0132 E-mail BPLord23@aol.com

Books

Bob and Penny Lord are authors of best sellers:

This Is My Body, This Is My Blood;
Miracles of the Eucharist Book I $9.95 Paperback
This Is My Body, This Is My Blood;
Miracles of the Eucharist Book II $13.95 Paperback
The Many Faces Of Mary, A Love Story $9.95 Paperback $13.95 Hardcover
We Came Back To Jesus $9.95 Paperback $13.95 Hardcover
Saints and Other Powerful Women in the Church $13.95 Paperback
Saints and Other Powerful Men in the Church $14.95 Paperback
Heavenly Army of Angels $13.95 Paperback
Scandal of the Cross and Its Triumph $13.95 Paperback
The Rosary - The Life of Jesus and Mary $13.95 Hardcover
Martyrs - They Died for Christ $13.95 Paperback
Visionaries, Mystics, and Stigmatists $13.95 Paperback
Visions of Heaven, Hell and Purgatory $13.95 Paperback
Treasures of the Church - That which makes us Catholic $9.95 Paperback
Tragedy of the Reformation $9.95 Paperback
Cults - Battle of the Angels $9.95 Paperback
Trilogy (3 Books - Treasure..., Tragedy... and Cults...) $25.00 Paperback
Journey to Sainthood - Founders, Confessors & Visionaries $10.95 Paperback
Holy Innocence - The Young and the Saintly $10.95 Paperback
Defenders of the Faith - Saints of the Counter-Reformation $10.95 Paperback
Super Saints Trilogy (3 Books - Journey ... Holy... Defenders...) $25.00

Please add $4.00 S&H for first book: $1.00 each add'l book

Videos and On-site Documentaries

Bob and Penny's Video Series based on their books:
13 part series on the Miracles of the Eucharist - 15 part series on The Many Faces of Mary - 23 part series on Martyrs - They Died for Christ - 10 part series on Visionaries, Mystics and Stigmatists - 50 part series on the Super Saints Trilogy
Many other on-site Documentaries based on Miracles of the Eucharist, Mother Mary's Apparitions, and the Heavenly Army of Angels. Request our list.
Our books and videos are available in Spanish also

Pilgrimages

Bob and Penny Lord's ministry take out Pilgrimages to the Shrines of Europe, and Mexico every year. Come and join them on one of these special Retreat Pilgrimages. Call for more information, and ask for the latest pilgrimage brochure.

Lecture Series

Bob and Penny travel to all parts of the world to spread the Good News. They speak on what they have written about in their books. If you would like to have them come to your area, call for information on a lecture series in your area.

Good Newsletter

We are publishers of the Good Newsletter, which is published four times a year. This newsletter will provide timely articles on our Faith, plus keep you informed with the activities of our community. Call 1-800-633-2484 for information.